Jesus: The Human Face of God

OTHER BOOKS BY JAY PARINI

Singing in Time (poems)

Theodore Roethke: An American Romantic (criticism)

The Love Run (novel)

Anthracite Country (poems)

The Patch Boys (novel)

An Invitation to Poetry (textbook)

Town Life (poems)

The Last Station (novel)

Bay of Arrows (novel)

John Steinbeck: A Biography

House of Days (poems)

Benjamin's Crossing (novel)

Some Necessary Angels: Essays on Literature and Politics

Robert Frost: A Life

The Apprentice Lover (novel)

One Matchless Time: A Life of William Faulkner

The Art of Teaching

The Art of Subtraction: New and Selected Poems

Why Poetry Matters (criticism)

Promised Land: Thirteen Books that Changed America

The Passages of H. M. (novel)

Jesus

THE HUMAN FACE
OF GOD

JAY PARINI

ICONS SERIES

New Harvest
Houghton Mifflin Harcourt
BOSTON • NEW YORK
2013

This edition published by special arrangement with Amazon Publishing

For information about permission to reproduce selections from this book,
write to Permissions, Houghton Mifflin Harcourt Publishing Company,
215 Park Avenue South, New York, New York 10003.

www.hmhbooks.com

Library of Congress Cataloging-in-Publication Data
Parini, Jay.
Jesus : the human face of God / Jay Parini.
pages cm
ISBN 978-0-544-02589-9
1. Jesus Christ — Biography. I. Title.
BT301.3.P37 2012
232.9′01 — dc23
[B]
2013001713

Book design by Brian Moore

Printed in the United States of America
DOC 10 9 8 7 6 5 4 3 2 1

Permission to quote from R. S. Thompson granted by
Orion Publishing Group.

For Devon
In the life of the spirit

Contents

Preface

Take my yoke upon you and learn from me, for I am
gentle and humble in heart, and you will find rest for
your soul. For my yoke is easy and my burden light.

— MATTHEW 11:29–30

The soul of man is the lamp of God.

— HEBREW PROVERB

THIS IS A BIOGRAPHY OF JESUS, not a theological tract, though I take seriously the message embodied
in the story of Christ that unfolded in real time. In *Jesus: The Human Face of God*, I offer a fresh look at him from the
viewpoint of someone (a poet, novelist, and teacher of literature) who regards scripture as continuous revelation, embodied
not only in the four gospels — still the main source for information about the life of Jesus — but also in extracanonical writing,
such as the Gnostic Gospels, as well as in centuries of poetry
and literature, where we see that prophecy remains active and
ongoing. I emphasize throughout what I call the *gradually realizing kingdom of God* — a process of transformation, like that of
an undeveloped photograph dipped in chemicals. The process
itself adds detail and depth to the image, which grows more distinct and plausible by the moment.

Literal-minded readings of the scriptures distort this understanding of the kingdom of God in unfortunate ways. In my

view, one is not "saved" by simply checking off the boxes in a code of dogmatic beliefs — this is not what Jesus had in mind. He asked more of us than that, and offered more as well. And so, in this portrait of Jesus's life and ideas, I put forward a *mythos* — a Greek word meaning story or legend — which suggests that the narrative has symbolic contours as well as literal heft, and that one should always read this story with a kind of double vision, keeping in mind the larger meanings contained in the words and deeds that have mattered so much to Christians over two millennia. Modern theologians have talked about demythologizing Jesus, but I want to remythologize him. At every turn in this biography, I try to imagine what Jesus meant to those who encountered him, and how his teachings and behavior inspired deeply personal transformations with public or social (even political) implications.

Jesus was a religious genius, and the Spirit moved in him in unique ways, with unusual grace and force, allowing him access to the highest levels of God-consciousness. His own life provided an example of how to behave in the world, urging us to love our neighbors as ourselves, to turn the other cheek when struck, and to remain fixed on "faith, hope, and love." "This is my commandment," Jesus said, putting before us a single ideal, "That you love one another, as I have loved you" (John 15:12). The simplicity and force of this statement take away the breath.

In the course of this book, I make an effort to place Jesus and his teachings within the context of desert wisdom. He came into this world at a turning point in history, a devout Jew trained in the laws of Moses and the traditions of Judaism. But he lived on the Silk Road, where he had access to Eastern as well as Western ideas. These currents informed his thoughts, and the Sermon on the Mount — where the core of his teaching lies in compressed form — extended and transformed key Jewish concepts while absorbing the Hindu and Buddhist idea of Karma: the notion that we ultimately reap what we sow. Jesus thought of the human mind in Greek terms, of course: an amalgam of body and soul. Yet his understanding of the human condition drew on every available concept as he set forth at the age of thirty with energy and passion, hoping to reshape the world, speaking not to elites — those who ruled the Roman Empire or administered the Second Temple in Jerusalem — but to the poor, the weak, and the marginalized. Here was, indeed, a revolution.

He was a ferocious, challenging teacher, hardly the Jesus "meek and mild" of the church hymn. And he made huge demands on those drawn toward him, as when he says in Mark 8:34: "Whoever will come after me, let him deny himself, and take up his cross, and follow me." It's an audacious invitation and one that Christians rarely take with the seriousness intended. The Way of Jesus, as it might be called, involves self-denial, a sense of losing oneself in order to find oneself, moving through the inevitable pain of life with good cheer, accepting gracefully the burdens that fall on our shoulders and the tasks that lie before us. This is true discipleship.

On this subject, I often recall the life of Dietrich Bonhoeffer, the German theologian and minister who was executed by the Nazis in a concentration camp at Flossenbürg on April 9, 1945, only a few weeks before its liberation by the Allies. Bonhoeffer stood up boldly to Hitler, and his anti-Nazi activities led to his arrest by the gestapo. During his imprisonment in Berlin's Tegel Military Prison for a year and a half, Bonhoeffer offered comfort and inspiration to his fellow prisoners, and even his Nazi jailors admired his courage and compassion, the example he set for others in a dire situation. He imitated Jesus there, making use of his example, allowing it to define his own life and actions.

Bonhoeffer reflected passionately on the meaning of his life, writing in his diary only a few months before his death: "It all depends on whether or not the fragment of our life reveals the plan and material of the whole. There are fragments which are only good to be thrown away, and others which are important for centuries to come because their fulfillment can only be a divine work. They are fragments of necessity. If our life, however remotely, reflects such a fragment . . . we shall not have to bewail our fragmentary life, but, on the contrary, rejoice in it."[1]

In *The Cost of Discipleship*, a bracing theological work, Bonhoeffer meditates at book-length on what it means to take up the cross: "Discipleship means adherence to Christ, and, because Christ is the object of that adherence, it must take the form of discipleship. An abstract Christology, a doctrinal system, a general religious knowledge on the subject of grace or on the forgiveness of sins, render discipleship superfluous, and in fact they positively exclude any idea of discipleship whatever, and are essentially inimical to the whole conception of following Christ."[2] So it won't do simply to follow a doctrinal system, marking off the things one has to believe in order to be "saved." To follow the Way of Jesus, one has to walk in a certain direction, experiencing the difficulties as well as the illimitable freedom of that choice. "Happy are the simple followers of Jesus Christ who have been overcome by his grace," writes Bonhoeffer. "Happy are they who, knowing that grace, can live in the world without being of it, who, by following Jesus Christ, are so assured of their heavenly citizenship that they are truly free to live their lives in this world."[3] Bonhoeffer's statement makes one question the idea of dogma, the notion that one should adhere to strict rules and prescribed statements in order to pursue the Christian way.

Jesus himself would have been startled to learn that, only a few centuries after his death — with the conversion of Emperor Constantine in the early fourth century — the Roman Empire itself would officially adopt his teachings and make them the law of the land. He might well have balked at the thought that a world religion would arise in his name, with competing theologians (and armies), all convinced that their understanding of his gospel message is correct, while other views are wrong. Jesus had no intention of founding a church (Greek: *ekklesia*) in competition with Judaism, although as the parable of the mustard seed suggests, he could imagine large numbers of people flocking to his tree of ideas like birds.

In the last chapter of this book, I explore the "afterlife" of Jesus, how a church gradually formed, with competing ideas about what his life meant. I also explore the various attempts to write about his life, which in the modern age began in the eighteenth century, when after the Enlightenment a degree of skepticism arose about the historical status of Jesus and the deeds and words relayed in the gospels. But that's later in the story. The starting point, for me — as suggested above — is the world into which Jesus was born, a pervasively Jewish world in Palestine at one of the major junctures in history, when the message that Jesus offered struck a small chord among a core group of people — most of them Mediterranean peasants who could barely read or write — that would grow louder and more resonant in time.

Yet questions loom: Who exactly was this man, Jesus of Nazareth? Was he, as some scholars argue, a wandering rabbi, a magician, a healer and exorcist like many others at this time, including Rabbinic sages such as Honi ha-Ma'agel or Hanina ben Dosa?[4] Was he also an apocalyptic visionary who imagined an end to history? As anyone who reads the gospels soon notices, Jesus quoted easily and often from Hebrew scriptures, with incredible alertness to parallels that foreshadowed his own story. He understood that Jews in Palestine felt profoundly uneasy under Roman rule, and he reflected this political reality in the things he said and did. But it's important to keep in mind that he was always a good, if unconventional, Jew. The fact that he took himself to be the long-awaited Christ (the Greek word for messiah) would, in fact, hardly have endeared him to Jewish authorities, who never imagined that the Chosen One would come from peasant stock in a remote Galilean village. That wasn't what they had in mind, and they looked askance at his purveyance of "signs and wonders" — miracles and astounding deeds that drew crowds wherever he went.

Christians have sometimes turned away from the supernatural aspects of his life with a sense of embarrassment. Walking on water? Giving sight to blind men? Healing lepers? Turning water into wine? Bringing the dead back to life? Rising from the dead after being crucified? Thomas Jefferson and Leo Tolstoy — both sons of the Enlightenment — sifted through the gospels with great care and a red pencil, underlining the aphorisms where his wisdom shone; at the same time, they crossed out the supernatural parts, including the Resurrection, which they assumed no self-respecting intellectual could abide. In *What Is Religion?* Tolstoy puts his views forward without fudging his skepticism: "Religion is not a belief, settled once for all, in certain supernatural occurrences supposed to have taken place once upon a time, nor in the necessity for certain prayers and ceremonies; nor is it, as the scientists suppose, a survival of the superstitions of ancient ignorance, which in our time has no meaning or application to life; but religion is a certain relation of man to eternal life and to God, a relation accordant with reason and contemporary knowledge."[5]

To this day liberal Christians tend to deflect the "superstitious" parts of the Jesus story and prefer to see religion as "a relation accordant with reason and contemporary knowledge," with Jesus as a prophet who preached love and nonviolent resistance to evil. He becomes simply a wise man who wished us to behave like the Good Samaritan in the parable (Luke 10:29–37), that kindly fellow who went out of his way to help a robbed and beaten traveler who lay by the roadside. This was ethical behavior of a high order, and Jesus encouraged such habits of rectitude and responsibility. Love your neighbor. Treat people as you would treat yourself (unless you happen to treat yourself badly).

This Jesus stands in contrast to the Jesus of evangelical Protestantism, where he becomes the Savior, the single doorway to heaven, the only route to eternal life, the way to ward off the flames of hell. Indeed, we're all familiar with the bumper sticker versions of this theology, perhaps best summed up as "Jesus Saves." For such Christians, the Redeemer was required by his father in heaven to die for the sins of humanity. In this tradition, simply believing that he gave his life for our sins buys admittance to God's kingdom. This is widely known as conversion: "Believe in the Lord Jesus Christ, and you will be saved, and your house," as we read in Acts 16:31. It's a simple idea, attractive to large numbers of people, although such a picture of Jesus and his "good news" tends to oversimplify his message and meaning, leading to a kind of limited vision that is both reductive and — in my opinion — dangerous. It suggests that one can, in an instant, cross a magical line and acquire salvation instead of entering into the gradually realizing kingdom of God, a process of daily transformation.

Jesus invited, even insisted on, a change of heart, asking us to repent. But repentance is only part of the deeper meaning buried in the Greek term *metanoia* — a key word in the New Testament. The word derives from *meta*, meaning "to move beyond," as in metaphysics, or "grow large or increase." *Noia* means "mental" or "mind." So the word, quite specifically, means: "to grow large in mind." When scriptures suggest that one should "repent" in order to be "saved," this actually means that in addition to having a change of heart — and that remains a core meaning here — one should go beyond the mind, reaching for awareness of the spirit, for a deep grounding in God. Even to be "saved" doesn't relate to "salvation" in the most common sense of the term: *soteria* in Greek. It means "being filled with a new spirit." In other words, one shifts consciousness, through prayer and meditation, through worship, seeking a larger and wider consciousness. One wakes up into the kingdom, moving beyond the deadening confines of everyday reality.

This is very different from the usual focus on repentance and salvation, concepts that actually derive from the early Church Fathers, especially Justin Martyr, who influenced Irenaeus and Tertullian, early theologians who focused on the need for remorse, for expiation — getting rid of one's sinful deeds by admitting them. St. Jerome, who translated the Bible into Latin in the late fourth century, absorbed this teaching, and he set in motion a range of theological misperceptions by translating *metanoia* as *paenitentia*, which becomes, in English, *repent*, as in the King James Version (KJV): "Repent ye, for the kingdom of heaven is at hand!" (Matthew 3:2).

This translation does not reflect a properly complex version of the term *metanoia* (which occurs fifty-eight times in the New Testament). The word itself suggests a beckoning by God toward the human soul, an invitation to spaciousness and awakening.[6] It implies a reaching beyond (*meta*) the mind (*noia*), a wish to acquire a wider spiritual awareness. A better way to translate this verse in Matthew would be: "Have a true change of heart and wake up to God. The spaciousness of his kingdom lies inside you. Transformation is not only possible: it lies within your grasp." This, for me, is what it means to be "saved," and it asks more of us than mere assent to a list of beliefs. It requires a mindfulness and absorption of God's kingdom that is, in the end, life changing.

While not a biblical scholar, I have over many years been in close contact with Christianity and Christians from different (often conflicting) theological traditions. Growing up in the home of a former Roman Catholic turned Baptist minister, I often sat through hot summer evenings in tabernacle meetings of a kind familiar to anyone who has watched Billy Graham on television. Indeed, I heard the Reverend Graham in person on more than one occasion, and countless times on television and radio — my family listened every Sunday at lunchtime to his weekly radio sermon. I continue to have genuine sympathy for what might be called "that old-time religion." Every morning at the breakfast table, my father read from the King James Version of the Bible, large portions of which I committed to memory. I later studied the Greek New Testament, reading a good deal of theology in college, graduate school, and beyond. Christian theology has been a preoccupation of mine for some five decades. (I should note that most of the versions of the New Testament quoted in this book are my own, produced by working from an interlinear Greek-English text. For reasons of familiarity I sometimes prefer the King James Version, as when I quote the Beatitudes or the Lord's Prayer. I use the KJV in all cases when quoting from the Hebrew scriptures. To my ear, it's what the Old Testament sounds like.) As a young man I became, and I remain, a member of the Episcopal Church, with an Anglican disposition — a consequence of ten years spent in Britain, perhaps.

My religious affections range widely, probably as a result of the mongrel past described above. At the University of St. Andrews, in Scotland, I wrote a graduate thesis on Ignatius Loyola, the founder of the Jesuit movement and an innovator in the field of devotional practice, as seen in his *Spiritual Exercises*, which dates to the early sixteenth century. In college, I was thoroughly enamored of modern theologians like Paul Tillich and Rudolf Bultmann, who brought my evangelical orientation into question; yet I retain a sympathy for the re-

ligion of my childhood: my heart warms when I hear hymns
like "Blessed Assurance" or "Just as I Am." My own religious
practice, however, draws on many strands in Christianity, and
my reading in the field ranges over any number of (often contradictory) spiritual writers, many of them as much influenced
by Buddhism as Christian theology. (I regularly teach a course
on poetry and spirituality at Middlebury College, bringing me
into constant contact with a range of spiritual writing from the
Psalms through the *Tao Te Ching*, the poems of Rumi, as well
as T. S. Eliot, R. S. Thomas, Charles Wright, and Mary Oliver,
among others. In fact, I write as someone who has spent more
time reading poetry than scholarly studies of Jesus.) Although
I will allude frequently to competing interpretations of biblical texts, my focus will remain on my own understanding of the
meaning of the life of Christ — provisional as this must necessarily be.

In the final chapter of this book, I attempt to deal with the
often contradictory efforts of scholars in recent centuries to locate the historical foundations of the Jesus story: the so-called
quest for the historical Jesus. It's not easy work, as the biblical
trail alone is often blurry, and the usual techniques of "scientific" history rarely apply here. The gospels themselves can't be
considered historical evidence in the modern sense of that term.
But in my attempt to reimagine the *mythos* of Jesus, I try to take
all this uncertainty into account, retelling the story as I see it,
noting the difficulties of interpretation where they arise, drawing attention to contradictions where they exist, while trying to
see Jesus steadily and whole through the kaleidoscopic lens of
many texts.

Now in my midsixties, I'm still in search of Jesus, and this
seeking often seems more important than the finding. To a large
degree, this biography itself represents the fruit of my decades-
long project of trying to understand Jesus and to take his example purposefully in my own life. I often recall some lines from

the *Gospel of Thomas*, one of the Gnostic Gospels discovered in the sands of Egypt at Nag Hammadi in 1945:

> *If you are searching,*
> *You must not stop until you find.*
> *When you find, however,*
> *You will become troubled.*
> *Your confusion will give way to wonder.*
> *In wonder you will reign over all things.*
> *Your sovereignty will be your rest.*[7]

This search, for me, involves a great deal of confusion, although it often gives way to wonder, to a feeling of all-embracing peace and sympathy for others. Jesus invites me to consider the lilies, and to understand that, by grace, I have access to a wider kingdom than I'd previously imagined. It's a matter of "thy will be done," not my own willing: a shift of emphasis that lifts the burden.

While I pay close attention to the facts in this biography of Jesus, the historicity of his life is less important than the meaning of the story itself. It doesn't matter what aspects of his life — his sayings, the exemplary deeds that formed the core of his ministry, the miracles — can be confirmed (or denied) by historians. At the end of his recent book, *Constructing Jesus*, Dale C. Allison, Jr. — a leading New Testament scholar — concludes his long study with a moving frankness: "While I am proudly a historian, I must confess that history is not what matters most. If my deathbed finds me alert and not overly racked with pain, I will then be preoccupied with how I have witnessed and embodied faith, hope, and charity. I will not be fretting over the historicity of this or that part of the Bible."[8] This rings true in my ears.

What matters is the way that God moved in the life of Jesus, who showed us how to find this spirit within ourselves.

Ralph Waldo Emerson put the matter succinctly in his "Divinity School Address," delivered at Harvard in 1838:

> Jesus Christ belonged to the true race of the prophets. He saw with open eye the mystery of the soul. Drawn by its severe harmony, ravished with its beauty, he lived in it, and had his being there. Alone in all history he estimated the greatness of man. One man was true to what is in you and me. He saw that God incarnates himself in man, and evermore goes forth anew to take possession of his world. He said, in this jubilee of sublime emotion, "I am divine. Through me, God acts; through me, speaks. Would you see God, see me."

The story of Jesus transcends time and physical boundaries. To understand it, one must remain open to every possibility, regarding the miracles of Jesus and the Resurrection as mysteries more alluring than frustrating, more inspiring than disconcerting. I narrate the life of Jesus from Bethlehem to Golgotha and beyond — with sympathy for its profound mythic pull, its transforming powers. I stop by the wayside to explain major moments or concepts that may not be familiar to all readers, such as the Virgin Birth or the Transfiguration. In the process of remythologizing Jesus, I take in stride the supernatural aspects of his life, believing that reality is more complex than we usually think, and that we can't begin to imagine the truth of things with the limited intellectual and perceptual machinery we've been given. In this, I follow St. Anselm, who referred to "faith on a quest to know," writing: "For I do not seek to understand so that I may believe, but I believe so that I may understand."

Within the Christian worldview, history becomes a pattern of timeless moments. And the work involves trying to find a place in the bewildering universe of hints and guesses that confront us as we search, looking around us at things we can

scarcely hope to comprehend with the limited intellect and resources we've been given. As T. S. Eliot put it so beautifully in
"The Dry Salvages":

> *These are only hints and guesses,*
> *Hints followed by guesses; and the rest*
> *Is prayer, observance, discipline, thought and action.*

I

Ancient Palestine

Jesus was a Near Eastern event.

— CYNTHIA BOURGEAULT, *The Wisdom Jesus*

The lines are fallen unto me in pleasant
places; yea, I have a goodly heritage.

— PSALM 16:6

Along the Silk Road

I RECENTLY STOOD AT sunrise on a hill overlooking Jerusalem, with goat bells tinkling in the middle distance. The Mount of Olives loomed in a rising mist, the air tinged with the odor of cypress, not unlike the smell of sage with a twist of lemon. It occurred to me that for thousands of years this prospect had remained more or less unchanged. This bleached landscape was a place where generations of merchants and caravans traveled along the Silk Road in search of wealth and adventure, where foreign armies came and went, where religious passions met, sometimes mingled, often clashed in near apocalypse. The walled city itself was a palimpsest, with many erasures and overwritten passages; it speaks of stratified cultures, layer upon layer: pagan, Jewish, Christian, Muslim, and many iterations of each. It has always, indeed, been a site of placement and displacement, sacred to someone, a major cross-roads between East and West, an incendiary point on any map of the world.

For good reason, theologians, historians, and archaeologists have focused intensely on Palestine, especially in the biblical period, and recent work has produced revelations that only enhance the mythic aspect of place in this land. Palestine is a magnet for *mythos*, the cradle of desert wisdom. And the narrative residue of this area is daunting: a thousand and one tales mingle here, true and partially true, fantastic or realistic. The degree to which ancient Hebrew scripture represents what actually occurred during the millennium before Jesus's birth, up through the day of his crucifixion in the third decade of the first century is, by itself, a subject that has vexed scholars over the centuries. Yet we know a great deal more about Palestine now than we did only a century ago. "It is no exaggeration to say that since the mid-twentieth century our Western map of the known Christian universe has been blasted wide open," writes Cynthia Bourgeault, a scholar who has looked closely at the wisdom tradition in the teachings of Jesus.[1] She refers mainly to the discovery of the Gnostic Gospels, such as the *Gospel of Thomas*, at Nag Hammadi in Egypt, as well as the Dead Sea Scrolls in Qumran. In fact, the doors and windows have been flung open by archaeology and textual criticism, and our knowledge of ancient Palestine has multiplied exponentially, bringing new perspectives on the life of Jesus.

A few points we can assume: Jesus was no illiterate carpenter without access to the marketplace of ideas. Living on the Silk Road, a trading thoroughfare between East and West, he would have encountered Hellenistic notions of the soul's immortality that poured in from the West, from Greece and Rome, and felt the heady winds of mysticism blowing from Persia and the East. Many cultural historians, such as Jerry H. Bentley, have dangled the possibility before us that Buddhism played a role in the shaping of early Christianity, with stories about the Buddha often having parallels in the life and teachings of Jesus.[2] At the very least, religion and trade were binding influences in Palestine at this critical juncture in time, and one can't overestimate the impact these had on ideas circulating in Galilee at the beginning of this millennium.

In short, the world into which Jesus was born during the time of Augustus Caesar was cosmopolitan as well as Jewish, if reluctantly under Roman authority. The emperor allowed any number of client kings to operate on its behalf: Herod the Great, for instance, kept an eye fixed on Rome for direction as he reigned over an impressive kingdom, where religious culture flourished, centered on the magnificent Second Temple in Jerusalem, which (according to Luke 2:39–52) Jesus visited with his family, who probably joined regular caravans from Nazareth, his home village, to worship at religious festivals, such as the feast of Passover.

This was a desert world alert to every spiritual wind that swept its bright and stony surfaces, a place with "an awesome, all-pervading sense of time and space," as Joseph Campbell, the great student of world myth, has noted, calling it "a kind of Aladdin cave within which light and darkness, spirit and soul, interplay to create" a world where the human and the divine mingled under the relentless sun. Campbell concludes: "The individual in this world is not an individual at all, but of an organ or part of the great organism — as in Paul or Augustine's view of the Living Body of Christ. In each being, as throughout the world cavern, there play the two contrary, all-pervading principles of Spirit and Soul."[3]

A Desert Society

Ancient Palestine stretched from the Mediterranean Sea to the Jordan River and adjoining territories: a landscape of ol-

ive and fig trees, juniper and date palms, fields of grain, vineyards, fragrant desert flowers and plants, undulating mountains
and fertile valleys, with sunlight shimmering off stone buildings — especially the magnificent Second Temple in Jerusalem,
which Herod (shortly before the birth of Jesus) enlarged to a
size nearly as big as his ego. It became the focal point for Jewish
worship, even for civic life in the capital. Indeed, the rebuilding
of the Second Temple involved large numbers of people over
several decades. According to Joachim Jeremias, a revered New
Testament scholar: "When the work began, 10,000 lay workers
and 1000 priests trained for the purpose are said to have been
engaged."[4] That's a small army. The historian Titus Flavius Josephus (37–100 CE), who remains a major source of information
about the early Christian era, described entering the Temple
himself and being dazzled by the golden façade that made him
blink with admiration and awe. Jeremias says: "Even though we
must take the statements of Josephus with critical caution, we
cannot doubt that the Temple was built with the greatest possible splendor and provided great opportunities for craftsmanship in gold, silver and bronze. Indeed, on entering the Temple,
no matter from what direction a man came, he would have to
pass through double gates covered with gold and silver."[5]

Jesus didn't enjoy such luxuries, being from a poor village
in Galilee, the son of a journeyman (Greek: *tekton*), perhaps a
carpenter or mason by trade: linguists continue to argue over
the exact meaning of that term. It's certain, however, that life
outside the Temple itself was anything but lavish for most Jews
in this era. They lived in houses of rough-cut stone with flat-
tiled roofs and unpainted wooden doors. The windows had no
screens, of course, so flies were daily companions. These crude
dwellings had packed-dirt floors and open courtyards where
family and friends gathered for meals and conversation in a
peasant society wedded to the agricultural rhythms of planting
and harvest times. In the course of any day, Jesus would have

seen chickens, sheep, cattle, oxen, camels, goats, horses, and donkeys. The city streets would often have been paved or cobbled, but this was mostly a land of dusty roads and dry, windswept vistas. The smell of dung lingered in the air.

Few people in Palestine at this time could read and write, though devout Jews listened to readings of the Hebrew scriptures, the Tanakh, which included the Pentateuch (or Torah) — the five books of Moses — as well as the Prophets. The so-called Writings, such as the Proverbs, Ecclesiastes, or Job, were later additions to the canonical Hebrew Bible, but they circulated among Jews along with a large quantity of Midrash, a kind of writing devoted to interpreting the meaning of scripture, especially its legal and ethical aspects. Jesus knew these texts well, as we see from his conversations as reported in the gospels, and regarded teaching as a central aspect of his mission: indeed, his followers often called him Rabbi or Teacher. As I noted before, he considered himself a devout Jew with ideas about reforming Judaism, not someone with designs on starting his own religion. It's significant that he never left a word of writing himself, which meant that his sayings and parables rode on the uncertain breeze of oral tradition, circulating like spores, taking root here and there.

His native language was Aramaic, a Semitic tongue commonly spoken in Palestine at this time, especially among Jews. (It was in the Canaanite family of languages). By the first century, Greek had become the lingua franca of the eastern Mediterranean, and this was true in Palestine as well, as it had been under the influence of Hellenistic culture since its conquest by Alexander the Great in the fourth century BCE. One assumes that Jesus had some knowledge of Greek, although we lack hard evidence for this. The Romans, who arrived in the middle of the first century BCE, preferred Latin for official purposes, but Latin was rare in the streets (though not unknown). From the trial of Jesus before Pontius Pilate, a Roman prefect, we can assume that Jesus spoke Latin, although his degree of fluency can't be known. In short, Palestine offered a very complex linguistic stew.

Close to home, Jesus had access to civilized culture. He could have walked to Sepphoris in less than an hour, this city of forty thousand inhabitants and the capital of Galilee, as it lay only a few miles to the northwest of Nazareth. It was the home of King Herod Antipas (until he moved his palace to Tiberias in the 20s CE, when Jesus would have been a young man), and the royal court brought visitors from far and wide. The city perched on the top of a mountain like a bird, hence the Hebrew name for it: Zippori, after *tzipor*, meaning "bird." As the discoveries of recent archaeology reveal, it was a wealthy metropolis: the elaborate mosaic floors and colonnaded, paved streets confirm this. It was a busy commercial center, with two markets where traders brought goods from far and wide: woven fabrics from the east, an array of earthenware pots, jewelry, oil for burning in lamps, wooden furniture, beer and wine, fresh fish and fowl, various meats and baked goods, seasonings that included cumin, garlic, coriander, mint, mustard, and dill. Both men and women walked about in loose-fitting tunics, although the men wore leather belts or cloth girdles. Sandals were made of leather and sold in the marketplace. Any number of coins circulated for currency, often minted in Sepphoris.

Of course a substantial sector of the population in Palestine labored in agricultural jobs in this era. They planted and reaped barley or grapes or cared for animals. A smaller group manned fishing boats or worked in what might be considered the clothing industry: weaving cloth for tunics, tooling leather for sandals and belts. Some labored in the olive-oil business, cultivating the orchards or pressing the olives themselves. A number of beekeepers could also be found, as honey was much prized in Palestine, then as now. One could also find a number of butcher shops in any small city or town, and meat from Palestine traveled as far as Athens. Luxury goods, too, attracted any number of specialists, such as jewelers and goldsmiths. Jesus would have been familiar with all of these professions, and he made use of many images from the everyday lives of working men in his parables.

The Cultural and Religious Setting

Galilee in the first century was charged with religious feelings, with competing groups of rabbis—Rabbi Hillel and Rabbi Shammai each founded traditions of biblical study and practice, often in competition for followers. Several devout sects flourished, including the Sadducees and the Pharisees, the Essenes, and the Zealots—the latter a group that didn't come fully into view until the Jewish revolt of 66 CE, although precursor movements certainly existed. (Jesus not only knew of these sects but possibly belonged to one of them, as Géza Vermes—a pioneering scholar of Judaism and its influence on Christianity—notes.)[6] Each of these sects of Judaism had elaborate rules and habits, although none of them emphasized "belief," as the term is commonly understood by Christians today. Judaism, then as now, was a religion of practice, not intellectual or emotional assent. You lived as a Jew, following the laws put forward in the Torah. The afterlife could take care of itself.

The Sadducees—the name alludes to Saduc, a legendary high priest during the time of King David—formed an elite of wealthy or influential Jews, including the priests and elders who presided over ritual life in the temple. A worldly group, they got along well with outsiders (travelers from Rome and Greece, Gaul, Egypt and elsewhere) and considered the Pharisees narrow-minded because of their fanatical adherence to Mosaic laws. One occasionally hears of them in the Bible, as when in Matthew 22:23 we read of certain members of this group approaching Jesus: "That same day the Sadducees, who say there is no resurrection, came to him with a question." In Acts 23:8 we hear that this group had no belief in angels or spirits. Their world was utterly material, focused on the here and now, the physical universe, where ritual mattered as a guide to ethical behavior. They welcomed foreigners into their midst, even non-Jews.

The Pharisees, as their name suggests (the root of the term means "set apart"), wanted nothing to do with outsiders (non-Jews or gentiles), and today they would be considered purists. They thought of themselves as "friends" (Hebrew: *haberim*) of the covenant made by God through Moses with the people of Israel. They first arrived on the scene in the second century before Jesus, and by the time of his public ministry had become a dominant voice in Judaism, with strict rules of admission that included a period when they had to prove their willingness to adhere to ritual laws.[7] They stressed the need to help the poor and asked their members to tithe, giving a tenth of their income to the poor. As opposed to the Sadducees, they believed in the resurrection of the dead and leaned toward prophecy—ideas and tendencies that would influence Jesus in his thinking. And yet Jesus was in conflict with them repeatedly, as when, in Matthew 15:1–3, they complained to Jesus about the behavior of his followers: "Why do your disciples transgress the tradition of the elders? For they don't wash their hands when they eat bread." Jesus couldn't abide such rules, and suggested to his disciples in Matthew 23:5 that the Pharisees did all their works "to be seen by men." That is, they were showing off, concerned with outward conformity, not inward transformation.

The Essenes and Zealots were lesser movements in Palestine at this time, but they appealed in various ways to Jesus and his followers. Like the Pharisees, the Essenes advocated Jewish separateness, which they took to an extreme, living in exclusive communities, pursuing repentance and ritual purification. Some lived in mountain caves at Qumran (where the Dead Sea Scrolls were discovered in the mid-twentieth century). They were ascetics who led disciplined, prayerful lives—the Jewish equivalent of monks and nuns. They believed in the human soul and the resurrection of the body, concepts that Jesus would reinforce in his teaching. (There was a branch of the Essenes, or an offshoot, centered in Egypt called the Therapeutae, who strongly encouraged celibacy as a sign of devoutness, even encouraging new followers to abandon their wives and families. They engaged in a practice not unlike psychological counseling, and so they could be considered the ancestors of our present-day therapists.) The Zealots, barely in evidence yet, were less spiritually adept and theoretical. They were political revolutionaries: guerrillas, in effect. (One of the disciples of Jesus, Simon, may have been a Zealot.) In response to what they regarded as Jewish humiliation by the Romans, they wished to drive these pagan invaders from their homeland. As one major scholar of Jewish history has said, "From Galilee stemmed all revolutionary movements," and these "so disturbed the Romans" that they put pressure on local authorities to repress them by whatever means.[8] Among the legendary heroes of rebellion was Judas the Galilean, a co-founder of the Zealots. When we think about the eventual crucifixion of Jesus by Roman authorities, it's worth recalling that he associated with people—rabble-rousers, in effect—who resisted foreign occupation. The Zealots never forgot how badly the Jews had been treated by foreign occupations, and they recalled the destruction of the First Temple with a special distaste for their humiliation at the hands of the Babylonians.

For Jews, the past wasn't really past. When the First Temple (or Solomon's Temple) was destroyed during the siege of Jerusalem in 587 BCE, significant parts of the Jewish population—largely the middle and upper classes, which numbered about ten thousand people—were swept into captivity by the Babylonian Empire, which vastly outnumbered them. The loss of the Temple—the center of Jewish spiritual and political life—was irreparable and seemed to contradict everything God had foretold in the Holy Scriptures about the triumph of

Israel over its enemies, forcing a crisis of confidence, even a crisis of faith. *Why had God done this to us?* Jews wondered. *Had he not made promises about our triumph?* From this crisis came many of the mournful psalms and lamentations of the Hebrew Bible. But one also saw the emergence of Ezekiel and Daniel, books of the Old Testament that embody the dream of a return to the homeland, with a theology of salvation in which a Davidic kingdom might be reestablished under the protective eye of God. (Notice that salvation for Jews was a political manifestation of God's kingdom on earth, not a personal matter, as with many Christians.)

Not surprisingly, it was during the long Babylonian exile that Jews began to conceive of an actual adversary to God, someone who had plotted against his grand scheme for the triumph of Israel, and his opposition helped to explain the trouble at hand. This oppositional figure — not especially terrifying in his first appearances — was called *Ha-satan*, meaning "the Adversary." "Although he was a fairly insignificant nuisance in the Hebrew scriptures, he grew in status in later Jewish literature," says Diarmaid MacCulloch, author of *A History of Christianity: The First Three Thousand Years*, "particularly among writers who were influenced by other religious cultures which spoke of powerful demonic figures." *Ha-satan* evolved into Satan, growing in stature during the early Christian era, especially in the Book of Revelation, where he stages a final assault on God's authority at the Battle of Armageddon. Needless to say, he also took a star turn through the Book of Job — one of the later books of the Hebrew scriptures.

In the wake of the Babylonian exile, for half a century, the First Temple lay in ruins. It was a devastating period but, in retrospect, a fallow time, during which fresh ideas from Greece poured into the region, ultimately affecting early Christian thought in the first century. Alexander the Great had seized control of Palestine and adjacent territories on his eastward expansion, and he opened Judaic doors to Greek philosophical thought while giving the Greek language a solid foothold in the Middle East that it would not relinquish for generations. The dualism of Plato, in particular, with its distinction between the body and the soul, was a legacy that influenced thinkers such as the apostle Paul, whose theological speculations became the foundation of Christian thought.[9] One hears the Hellenistic note, for example, in the idea of "emptying out" or *kenosis* — the word Paul chooses in his jaw-dropping theoretical effusions in the second chapter of Philippians: "Do nothing out of personal ambition or self-regard but in humbleness regard others as more important than yourself. Let all of you look not only to your own interests but to the interests of others. Have the mind of Christ in yours, thinking of him, who (though he was a god) didn't consider his equality with God something he could attach himself to. Instead, he emptied himself out, taking on the form of a servant, having been born in the likeness of a man. And he humbled himself further, to the point of death on the cross. For this, God raised him up." Even here, in my reading, I detect echoes of the rebuilding of Solomon's Temple, that note of exile, a sense of Paul grappling with Greek ideas in original ways, shaping them to his own theological purposes.

Jesus benefited from the eclectic mix of ideas in Palestine during his coming of age. Yet it could not have been easy for him or any other devout Jew during the Roman occupation at the beginning of the first century, when there were strenuously competing notions about the nature and worship of God and the proper forms that religious practice should take. As the Talmudic scholar Daniel Boyarin recalls: "There were no rabbis yet, and even the priests in Jerusalem and around the temple were divided among themselves. Not only that, but there were many Jews both in Palestine and outside of it, in places such as Alexandria and Egypt, who had very different ideas about what being a good, devout Jew meant."[10] For his part, Jesus — a man with remarkable skills of spiritual intuition — had his own ideas, and these often conflicted with those of more conventional Jews, especially his notion of self-sacrifice: giving up the ego, allowing God to control our lives. "Blessed are the meek," he would say, "for they shall inherit the earth" (Matthew 5:5). Before this, one would have to look hard to find anyone celebrating "the meek" or suggesting that they would inherit anything at all, let alone "the earth."

In a unique fusion, Jesus gathered up many of the loose ends of Judaism, which had frayed badly in Palestine during this era. In a sequence of disruptive sayings and parables, some of which had their origins in Judaic thought and some from elsewhere, he set before the world an ethical code with visionary force, with the power to transform lives and society in spiritual and material ways. But he would do more than that, taking on the role of Messiah or (the Greek word for it) Christ: a luminous figure who became the ultimate symbol of suffering, death, and resurrection. It's not for nothing that we begin counting a new era from the date of his birth: Anno Domini, meaning the year of our Lord. But he came not only to provide comfort and ethical guidance, but to challenge those around him in ferocious, unsettling, even frightening ways. As T. S. Eliot put it so well in "Gerontion": "In the juvescence of the year / Came Christ the tiger."

2

In the Beginning

God became like us so that we might become like God.
— ST. ATHENASIUS, *De Incarnatione*

Aren't we enlarged
by the scale of what we're able
to desire?
— MARK DOTY, "Messiah"

THE EARLY CHRISTIANS HAD little information about the circumstances of Jesus's birth, and curiosity must have overwhelmed them. The first Christian writings — the letters of Paul (written perhaps two decades after the Crucifixion) — say nothing about Christmas or the birth of Jesus; indeed, Paul shows no interest whatsoever in the life of Christ, his origins, or his family life. The earliest gospel, Mark, makes no mention of the birth whatsoever. Neither does the author of John appear to have any knowledge of Christmas. Instead, that gospel famously opens with a philosophical speculation about Jesus being present before anything else in the form of *logos*, a Greek term that has no decent equivalent in English, though it's rendered as "Word" in nearly all translations: "In the beginning was the Word, and the Word was with God, and the Word was God" (John 1:1). The emphasis here lies in the notion of *logos* as an all-governing principle of creation permeating created things. But this is hardly like the Christmas story, which is much less philosophical and abstract.

Christmas is, by contrast, a legendary tale about a threatened family. A messenger of God comes to Mary, a terrified young virgin, and informs her that she would conceive a son without having slept with her husband-to-be, Joseph. The story soon becomes a narrative of dislocation and poverty: Jesus is born in a manger in Bethlehem, with his parents on the road, away from home. It's a story with obvious political implications, too, as Jesus — a marginal Jew born in meager circumstances — nevertheless seems to threaten the maniacal King Herod, who didn't want a rival for kingship of the Jews, and so he tried to get rid of this potential rival by killing all young male children in the region — a mythical event known as the Massacre of the Innocents. So the family is forced to hide in Egypt, adding the element of flight and fear to the story. But it's also a charming and magical account, with alluring imagery that sticks in the mind: a star hovers over the barn where Jesus lies, marking the spot of his emergence into history. Wise Men or Magi come from the east, traveling with gifts, on camels. Shepherds keep watch over their flocks by night, while the desert is cold, glistening on the eve of the Messiah's birth. The event happens at the winter solstice, when the world grows still in icy weather, only to open up and begin to move again, slowly, as it leans toward hope in the form of a baby, who arrives with the holy hush of amazement.

Only Luke and Matthew include Christmas in their narratives of the life of Christ, perhaps reformulating legends that had spread by word of mouth for many years, and their versions of the birth of Jesus sit uncomfortably together, with many contradictory elements. It's possible that these accounts arose gradually, in the decades after the death of Jesus, in different communities, and so the stories emphasize unique aspects of the tale, deepening the legend in ways that spoke to their present needs, as followers of Jesus, as threatened and marginal communities of faith who struggled to make sense of the man whose gospel or "good news" informed their lives.

The foregrounding moment in this tale is the Annunciation, a point at the beginning of the tale where Mary (and also Joseph, although separately) get a surprise visit from the angel Gabriel — a spirit mentioned only in the Book of Daniel before this startling appearance to Mary in the quiet of her chamber. Gabriel explained calmly to this young virgin that she would bear a special son. The angel speaks with a respectful brightness: "Hail, you that are highly favored, the Lord is with you: blessed are you among women" (Luke 1:38). This appearance, and the astonishing message of Gabriel, terrified the poor girl. Yet Gabriel told her not to be afraid but to celebrate: "You have found favor with God." (This favor was the "grace" we associate with Mary, as in "Hail Mary, full of grace," although the phrase comes from a misreading of the Latin translation of the Bible: the Greek word *kechoritomene* simply means "favored one.")[1]

The Annunciation has a wondrous quality about it, and it has been touchingly rendered in paintings by many of the greatest artists of the West, often with challenging interpretations of the scene, as in Fra Angelico's bold fresco at the San Marco convent in Florence (finished in 1445), where Mary is no meek teenager frightened by her situation and wishing to withdraw; rather, she stares with a frank boldness into the eyes of Gabriel, fully composed and taking on her fate as the person who will deliver God's child to the world. She seems proud, even delighted, by the fact that God singled her out as "handmaid of the Lord." Her crucial moment in history has come, and she seems equal to the task at hand.

The contradictions in the two birth narratives emerge with the genealogies that Matthew and Luke offer, as a way of establishing the pedigree of Jesus. In Matthew, the lineage begins

with Abraham — the ultimate Jewish patriarch of the Old Testament — and moves to David, a triumphant Jewish king, then
pivots through a sequence of royal Jewish names. This seems in
keeping with the Jewish slant on Jesus generally offered in that
gospel, as it stresses the Judaic heritage of the Christ child. Luke,
on the other hand, offers a lineage that would appeal to gentiles as well as Jews: Jesus's ancestry starts with Adam, father of
all mankind, and not Abraham, a shift of emphasis that brings
Jesus into a larger family that included gentiles. David is still
there, but the line runs this time through the prophets, suggesting a more spiritual kingdom than the one that Matthew had in
mind.

In both narratives, Mary gives birth to Jesus in Bethlehem.
No doubt it meant something to early Jewish followers of Jesus that Bethlehem should be the birthplace of their beloved
rabbi, as this small city on the West Bank of the Jordan was the
home of Jesse, father of David. It's a place where David had once
kept sheep and eventually was crowned King of Israel. Unlike
Nazareth, probably the real birthplace of Jesus, it had huge symbolic import. One recalls that when Philip, a disciple of Jesus,
explained to Nathanael that Jesus was the Messiah foretold by
Moses, Nathanael asked in a withering voice: "Can any good
thing come out of Nazareth?" (John 1:43–46). It's also significant that in the Old Testament one hears that a future shepherd
of the flock of Israel would emerge from Bethlehem (Micah
5:1–14). So it was fitting that the birth of Jesus should be associated with a holy place.

In Matthew, the Christmas story morphs into a tale of displacement, fear, and flight, with the Holy Family escaping into
Egypt, a thrilling but scary narrative. In Luke, a very different
kind of story unfolds. Joseph and Mary have been forced to
travel from Nazareth in Galilee to Bethlehem in Judea because
of a Roman census that is never even mentioned in Matthew.[2]
It's not obviously a dangerous situation. Indeed, Herod does

not threaten male children in Luke, nor do Jesus, Mary, and Joseph rush away to Egypt to escape the vengeance of Herod and his desire to murder a rival to his throne. It's an altogether more comforting story, easier on the ears of children, if less riveting.

The discrepancies in the Christmas narratives don't matter, not unless one feels an urgent need to regard these texts as literal truth, the infallible Word of God (not unlike the Koran in fundamentalist Islam). Each account of the Christmas story has its unique emphasis, with Matthew putting forward the concept of Jesus as royalty, in both his lineage and the notion that people of importance (the Magi) would come from far away to worship at his feet. Herod's sense of rivalry is also important in Matthew. He is a royal person, after all, if only in a spiritual way, and his presence in the world has political consequences, for himself and others. Luke, on the other hand, emphasizes the ordinary aspects of Jesus, his position as a marginal person. He is the son of Adam and the "Son of Man" as much as "Prince of Peace" or "Son of God."[3] Poor folk — shepherds are nothing if not poor — come to visit the manger, not Magi bearing fancy gifts.

Yet Luke is a wonderful writer, adding scenes that intensify the mythic echo chamber of the story. He says, for example, that after Mary became pregnant, she paid a three-month visit to her cousin Elizabeth in Hebron, in the hill country south of Jerusalem. Elizabeth was an old and previously barren woman. Her husband was Zacharias, an elderly priest of the temple, who learned from an angel that his wife was pregnant. (This visit to Zacharias mirrors a similar visit to Joseph, who has never gotten much attention for having been told by an angel that Mary's child would be someone special.) Zacharias actually doubted the news about his wife's pregnancy. How could such a thing happen at their age? Never one for skepticism, God struck Zacharias dumb, though he later regained his powers of speech upon the birth of his son: a symbolic restoration. The angel instructed Elizabeth that her son should be named John, and he in due course became John the Baptist. The narrative pointedly foreshadows a later story in the gospels, where John precedes Jesus as a prophet and religious teacher, then baptizes him in the Jordan River. And so the birth of John prefigures the birth of the Incarnate Word, Jesus: the spirit made flesh. John himself becomes "a voice crying in the wilderness."

Elizabeth understood Mary's situation at a glance. She intuited that the Holy Spirit, not Joseph, had created this child in her cousin's womb, and she understood that Mary would deliver the Son of God to the world. She cried out with a kind of giddy appreciation: "Blessed are you among women, and blessed is the fruit of your womb" (Luke 1:42). Mary replied eloquently and modestly, lowering her eyes to the floor: "My soul does magnify the Lord." Her response echoes in history, and the words have been set frequently to music, called the Magnificat after the Latin version of Mary's statement, which begins: *Magnificat anima mea Dominum.*[4]

The concept of the Virgin Birth, a miraculous event, means a great deal to Christians as a sign from God that the spirit was sent to dwell in human form. Yet it's worth recalling that the word "virgin" had an elastic meaning in both Greek and Hebrew. "It was certainly not confined to denoting men and women without experience of sexual intercourse," notes Vermes. "The Greek word could explicitly or implicitly include this meaning, or the main stress could fall on the youth of a girl or boy, and generally, though not necessarily, on their unmarried state."[5] In *The Masks of God*, Joseph Campbell observes: "On the level simply of legend, without regard to the possibility of an actual miracle, the Virgin Birth must be interpreted as a mythic motif from the Persian or Greek, not Hebrew, side of the Christian heritage."[6] Judaism, with its love of patriarchy, could not easily have generated a story in which the Messiah was not really one of Abraham's full-blooded sons.

Exactly what the gospel writers meant by proclaiming Mary's virginity has preoccupied theologians down the centuries as they have tried to understand or tease out its many possible implications. What is not in dispute among Christians is the more general idea that Jesus was no ordinary man, and that from conception he carried within his soul the spark of God, as in the word "Immanuel," which means "God dwells within," a name first mentioned in Isaiah 7:14, "Therefore the Lord will give you a sign: the young maiden will give birth to a son, and he will be called Immanuel." And the Virgin Birth anchors the Christmas story, putting forward a theological point of considerable subtlety as well as force.

Despite the lack of any reference to it elsewhere in the entire New Testament, the Virgin Birth remains a central tenet of Christian dogma, one developed by the Church Fathers — those early, highly influential, theologians and teachers, such as Origen, Tertullian, and Augustine. Sensing the lack of scriptural authority for the concept, the authors of later apocryphal gospels, such as the *Infancy Gospel of James*, often focused on the subject of Mary's virginity, suggesting that she remained a virgin even *after* her marriage to Joseph. The fact that Jesus had siblings, however, complicated the matter. Was Mary *not* their mother? These siblings may, of course, have been half siblings from an earlier marriage or, perhaps, cousins. Theologians have argued as much. But Matthew 13:55 states firmly that Jesus had at least four brothers (James, Joseph, Simon, and Judas) and two unnamed sisters. None of this contradicts the idea that Jesus was Mary's first child or that he didn't come from Joseph, but of God — at least in a symbolic way.

The rather fantastic idea that a human being might give birth to a child created by a god would have puzzled no one in the ancient world. Important people were often thought to be part human, part divine: Romulus and Remus, for example, the mythical twins who founded Rome, were the children of Rhea

Silvia and the god Mars. It was frequently said that Augustus, the great emperor, was conceived in the Temple of Apollo, with no human father. Modern readers with any knowledge of pagan mythology will be familiar with the concept of gods mingling with human beings, sometimes with astounding consequences, as when Leda was raped by Zeus in the form of a swan, producing an offspring named Helen, who would become Helen of Troy, that extraordinary beauty whose face, according to the poet Christopher Marlowe, "launched a thousand ships" and led to the Trojan War.

Just to note: the Virgin Birth should not be confused with the Roman Catholic idea of the Immaculate Conception, the doctrine that Mary was a human being and yet conceived without sin (Latin: *macula*), and therefore Jesus was not born to someone who had been tainted by the transgressions of Adam and Eve in the Garden of Eden, relating back to the doctrine of original sin, which simply means that every human being is stained by the sins of their original parents. But this lurches into the wilder thickets of theological speculation. What matters in the Christmas story is that Jesus should have come into the world in a way that conveyed a sense of his unique connection to God as well as his deep-seated humanity. The Virgin Birth, as a mythical concept, delivers that message quite beautifully.

It's worth dwelling on the story of the Magi, told with compression and charm in Matthew 2:1–12. "In the time of King Herod, after Jesus was born in Bethlehem of Judea, wise men from the East came to Jerusalem, asking *Where is the infant who has been born king of the Jews? For we saw his star rising, and have come to pay him homage.*" The star actually hovers over the stable where the child lies, suggesting to many in later years that these wise men could have been astrologers, who read meaning into stars and their patterns. "On entering the house, they saw the infant with Mary his mother; and they knelt down and paid him homage. Then, opening their treasure baskets, they offered

him gifts of gold, frankincense, and myrrh. And having been
warned in a dream not to return to Herod, they went back to
their own country by a different path."

This unlikely visit forms a haunting piece of narrative, often depicted by painters and framed with idiosyncratic perfection in T. S. Eliot's "Journey of the Magi." In this poetic mono-
logue, one of the wise men revisits the miraculous event years
afterward, remembering a journey undertaken in the "very dead
of winter." It had been a "cold coming" over icy mountains: a
journey from the old world of faithlessness and uncertainty to
the new world, where redemption and new life seemed at last
possible. The three Magi may well have been "holy Zoroastrian
astronomers," as E. F. Burgess speculated, suggesting they were
used to following the signs of heaven. The "Yonder Star" that
drew them to the West "was a sign prophesied 600 years before
by Zoroaster. The prophecy not only described the celestial occurrence, but also specifically named Bethlehem as the birthplace of the new prophet."[7]

The Magi have lodged themselves in the Western imagination, where names soon attached to them: Melchior, Cas-
par, and Balthasar. That they came "from the east" has within
it a sense of the rising sun, the beginning of a new day. In various Christian traditions, the wise men traveled from Babylon,
Persia, or Yemen. The actual number of Magi is never stated in
Matthew, but since they brought three gifts, they are commonly
imagined as a trio. The gifts they bring seem to acknowledge the
royalty at hand, and this follows Matthew's efforts to make the
Jesus into a princely child, with a Davidic heritage. And there
is the added sense of fulfilling Old Testament prophecies, as in
Isaiah 60:3: "And the Gentiles shall come to thy light, and kings
to the brightness of thy rising."

The gifts they bring have symbolic radiance. Gold was then,
as now, the most valuable of metals, the standard for wealth
from time immemorial, fit for a king. Frankincense was a cov-

eted perfume associated with temple rituals. And myrrh was a kind of oil, used for anointments and during the process of embalming. (It was later used in the Eastern Orthodox Church for major sacramental rites, such as confirmation or extreme unction — the last rites of the Church, which are bestowed upon the dying.) It was also widely believed in Jewish tradition that royalty would visit the infant who would become the Messiah, and the writer of Matthew understood the significance of this homage, that the Magi stand in for all yearning Christians, those who lean to beginnings, in search of the child who will bring light to the world in a dark time.

Even with all of its gleaming details, the Christmas story leaves a lot to the imagination, which is why in subsequent centuries the followers of Jesus filled in the blanks wherever possible, making the myth as concrete as they could. Neither Matthew nor Luke, for instance, specified the date of Jesus's birth — the calendar year would have been different in any case. Christians didn't settle on December 25 as Christmas Day until the fourth century, and this choice probably had something to do with its proximity to the winter solstice or its position as the final day of the Roman Saturnalia. It was in the late third century, in fact, that the Roman emperor Aurelian established this date as a feast day celebrating the birth of the Unconquered Sun (*Sol Invictus*), so it already had festive and quasi-religious prominence.[8] The Unconquered Sun becomes the Son of God, who conquers death itself.

After Christmas

What followed the manger scene in Bethlehem varies in Luke and Matthew, as noted above. In Matthew, the family in due course returns to Nazareth after the flight to Egypt, once the coast is clear. The flight itself, as Matthew wished to emphasize, fulfilled a prophecy in the Hebrew scriptures (Hosea 11:1),

where we read that a future leader will come "out of Egypt."
Such a twist in the narrative may have been added to underscore
the *Jewish* inheritance of Jesus as well as to amplify the mythic
reverberations of the story. The echoes between the flight to
Egypt and the legendary flight of the Jews into Egypt during
the period known as the Exodus were intentional. As ever, Matthew had a Jewish audience in mind, and his readers would hear
the reverberations in his telling. Herod wished to get rid of the
child who might be a future king of the Jews much as the Pharaoh (Exodus 2:15) wanted to get rid of Moses, issuing a bloody
command (1:22) that every Jewish male baby be thrown into the
Nile. God instructed Joseph, father of Jesus, in his dreams how
to proceed in difficult circumstances, perhaps reminding readers that Joseph's namesake in Exodus possessed the gift of interpreting dreams: so much so that his talent attracted the eye of
Pharaoh (Genesis 37:19; 41:25).

Matthew's Egyptian episode fascinated later writers, as we
see in the Apocrypha and Gnostic Gospels — material excluded
by makers of the official canon, yet fascinating to read. In one of
these, palm trees bow down before the progression of the infant
Jesus — an image of such brightness that it somehow lodged in
the Koran (19:25). In some versions of the flight to Egypt, a patient nurse called Salome looks after the child, and some regard
her as the sister of Mary; indeed she is occasionally thought to
be the Mary who appears beside Mary Magdalene at the foot of
the cross in Matthew 27:55, though once again the gospel narratives lack enough specificity to make such an identification.
Names, in fact, presented a constant problem for later generations of readers, who couldn't be sure that a particular name in
the New Testament attached to someone with the same name
elsewhere.

After his birth, Jesus would have been circumcised on the
eighth day, in accordance with Jewish custom; the eight days
symbolize the willingness of Abraham to sacrifice his son Isaac

on the eighth day. Luke mentions that Jesus was circumcised, dwelling on the ritual presentation of the child at the Temple (Luke 2:22–40). In this memorable scene, an elderly man called Simeon the Righteous steps into the picture from the wings, thrilled to see the Messiah before he dies. He was possibly one of the temple elders from the tribe of Levi who would have been authorized to bestow on the child the usual blessing for such occasions: "The Lord bless thee and keep thee, the Lord make his face to shine upon thee and be gracious unto thee, the Lord lift his countenance upon thee, and give thee peace" (Numbers 6:24–26). With relief and delight, he lifted the child in his arms, telling God that he could "now dismiss" him from this world. He offers a remarkable prayer of thanks known as the Nunc Dimittis, meaning simply "Now dismiss." It opens movingly: "Now Lord, let your servant go in peace." Another devout person in the temple at the time was Anna, referred to as a "prophetess" and remembered as a kind of godmother to Jesus. (Her name could also be translated as Hannah, echoing the story in Samuel where the prophetess Hannah gave birth to Samuel, another blessed child who would play a pivotal role in the history of the Jews.)

The ritual of purification happened forty days after the birth of the child in keeping with Jewish law (as framed in both Leviticus and Exodus). As required by law and custom, the parents of the newborn child sacrificed a pair of turtledoves (young pigeons) — no doubt because they could not afford to sacrifice a lamb.[9] Here, as elsewhere, readers must choose which tradition to follow, Matthew or Luke. If Jesus and his family had fled to Egypt from Bethlehem, as Matthew suggests, he would never have gone to Jerusalem for Mary's ritual purification, though literal-minded readers find ways to reconcile these stories.

Reconciliation is unnecessary, however, as anyone who engages Christianity in liturgy and practice will know; the Christmas story requires no defense. It represents the moment when the timeless enters time, when God begins a grand process of revelation. The star hovering over the manger in Bethlehem beckons, and the notion of wise men, or Magi, coming from the east to pay homage to the Christ child feeds our sense of expectation; we, like them, embark on a journey without a guarantee of arrival, bearing the gift of our own hope. And every year, as the holiday looms in late December, the urge to sing out in adoration comes. As the poet George Herbert wrote in the seventeenth century: "The shepherds sing; and shall I silent be?"

The Hidden Years

We know nothing about Jesus during the years of childhood, adolescence, and young manhood except for a slight but intriguing story in Luke 2:41–52. This glimpse of him involves his conversation with Temple elders in Jerusalem, at the age of twelve, offering a look at his developing character. It gives us an opportunity to see how Jesus regarded himself — and was viewed by others — at the doorstep of manhood.

The family — Mary, Joseph, Jesus, and his siblings — traveled to Jerusalem on their annual pilgrimage to the Second Temple. This edifice would have dazzled the young man: fifteen stories in height, with a profusion of gold ornamentation on a foundation of glistening limestone blocks called ashlars. The Wailing Wall — still in place — was its western foundation, and it's all that remains of the original edifice. It was actually a sequence of interlocking spaces that included rooms for prayer, worship, and study. Rabbinical courts met there as well, including the Sanhedrin. Like the Egyptian pyramids, Herod's Temple was a wonder of the world, grander than anything in Rome itself. That Mary and Joseph would come to Jerusalem to visit the Temple says something about their piety and spiritual ambitions. Being a *tekton*, or carpenter, Joseph ranked low — even a peasant with a little bit of land had more clout in society. Yet the family must have had the support of the Nazarene Jewish community. One assumes that Mary and Joseph traveled as part of a company of faithful Jews who made this three-day journey along dusty roads, traveling in a caravan, taking plenty of food and water, with some of the pilgrims riding on camels or donkeys. They would have passed through the lush Galilean countryside into the barren hills of Judea, edging along high cliffs as they approached the Holy City, with its amber walls, no doubt joining a throng that moved toward Jerusalem for the high holidays.

Jesus and his family would have entered the Temple through a grand entrance on the southern slope, which archaeologists have uncovered. It contained a series of bathing pools or *miqvaoth* that pilgrims used for ritual purification before entering the presence of God. One would have heard singers from the tribe of Levi chanting hymns from the Book of Psalms. One then approached the esplanade of the Great Court, under a series of broad porticos. The interior courtyards were reserved for Jews who had been purified in a ritual fashion. The final approach led to the Holy of Holies, the most sacred place in Judaism, which once (during the First Temple period) contained the Ark of the Covenant. Of course neither Jesus nor his family would have seen this holy place, which the High Priest himself could only approach one day a year (on Yom Kippur — the Day of Atonement, when blood was sprinkled on the altar).

After a week of celebrations that included gatherings for prayer, the sacrificing of animals, ritual bathing, and attendance at readings of Holy Scripture, the family of Jesus began their journey back to Nazareth. In the shuffle of their departure, Jesus got left behind, and his parents hurried back to look for him. It would have been terrifying for them, as anything might happen in a strange city. For two days they searched for their child without luck. On the third day they found him in the Temple, where he sat in a circle of elders and discussed the meaning of scriptures—the gospel doesn't give much detail here, although it would have been highly unusual to see a child of this age in such august circumstances and being taken seriously by the elders at hand. Jesus seems to have been precocious as well as devout and wildly self-confident. Mary, however, was not impressed by this spectacle, and she asked her son how he could act in such an inconsiderate manner. He replied, in a tone that still rings with a shock: "Don't you know I must be about my father's business?" As we read in Luke 2:50: "And they didn't understand what he said to them."

Jesus reluctantly deferred to his mother, who had apparently not fully absorbed yet that her child was God's own son. He went with his parents back to Nazareth and "was subject unto them," fulfilling the commandment to obey one's father and mother. (A later writer may have added this reassuring verse, feeling uncomfortable with this adolescent rebellious streak in Jesus.) During the years of his public ministry, however, Jesus urged his disciples to abandon their homes and to put everyone and everything to one side in pursuit of God's will for them. Family did not come first, not in his own life, even as a boy of twelve. He was obviously not easy for his parents to control, and it's probably a good thing that we hear little about him in Nazareth until he reemerges as a grown man.

This anecdote has another purpose, giving us a sense that Jesus was a scholar at heart. From an early age, he devoted himself to studying the scripture, and he enjoyed discussing the meaning of various passages. This seems right for one who would, in due course, become a model teacher, a man addressed by his followers as Rabbi, which means "a teacher of Torah," one grounded in Jewish law, the *halakha*. In fact, during the years of his public ministry, Jesus wandered through Galilee and adjacent territories with a notable aura of mission, offering his own readings of familiar Hebrew texts, attracting large crowds, who found his teachings both uplifting and convincing, if at times challenging and even heretical. This radical teacher is, in fact, an adult version of the twelve-year-old boy in the Temple.

The paucity of stories about the young Jesus frustrated early Christians, but any number of apocryphal evangelists took up the subject with relish, trying to fill in gaps. Over twenty more gospels have been found, sometimes in fragmentary form in languages such as Syriac and Armenian as well as Greek.[10] In many of the anecdotes associated with this extracanonical literature, Jesus takes the form of a trickster child-god from mythology, performing astounding (often silly) miracles. In one of them, for instance, he turns a salt cod into a live fish, scaring the wits out of his boyish companions. Elsewhere, he forms a number of birds from raw clay and then brings them to life with a sweep of the hand: *voilà!* In another, he shows a command of the alphabet that astonishes his teachers. But there is a dark side, too, as in the *Infancy Gospel of Thomas*, where he blinds the parents of a child who offends him — a bizarre and cruel act that seems calculated to make readers dislike or fear him. (One assumes, perhaps, that the writers of these gospels projected their own angers or frustrations onto this fantasy version of Jesus, which the church firmly rejected. Indeed, the Gospel of John states clearly that the miracle of changing water into wine at the wedding in Cana was Jesus's *first* miracle.)

So where was Jesus during his first thirty years, and how did he spend his time? One easily imagines him working with his father, perhaps in nearby Sepphoris, helping to build a theater or colonnade or sports arena. It's obvious that he studied the Hebrew Bible at his local synagogue, as his later ministry reveals an intimate knowledge of these texts. He might have spent time working in nearby vineyards or barley fields, as his later teachings often rely on pastoral images, perhaps gleaned from childhood. His geographical horizon was limited, a point that emerges when he commands his followers to witness for him "in Jerusalem, and in all Judaea, and in Samaria, and to the outermost parts of the earth" (Acts 1:8). The likelihood is that Jesus never left Palestine, although folklore has placed him as far afield as India. The notion that Jesus visited England was prevalent, too, as we see when William Blake asks: "And did those feet in ancient time / Walk upon England's mountains green?" The answer, alas, is: *No.*

The hidden years in the life of Jesus remain unrecoverable, the stuff of legend, most of it fanciful. No doubt he underwent many of the same transformations, sexual and personal, that occur within the body and mind of any adolescent. He grew in knowledge of the world and, in his case, vastly increased his spiritual awareness. "That he, like every human being, struggled toward some definition of self within, in relation to, and perhaps in opposition to, larger social units is equally clear," writes John P. Meier in *A Marginal Jew*, a major four-volume study of Jesus and his teachings.[11] Yet Jesus came into full public view only in young adulthood, after his baptism in the Jordan River by John the Baptist, when the heavens opened for him, and he experienced a transformation from Jesus to Messiah or Christ: one fully realized in his ministry, his death, and his ultimate resurrection.

3

The Dove Descending: His Ministry Begins

> To his great baptism flocked
> With awe the regions round, and with them came
> From Nazareth the son of Joseph deemed
> To the flood Jordan — came as then obscure,
> Unmarked, unknown.
>
> — JOHN MILTON, *Paradise Regained*

The One Who Goes Before

THE PUBLIC LIFE of Jesus began with his baptism in the Jordan River. He came, as it were, out of nowhere, a young man from Nazareth: "obscure, / Unmarked, unknown," as Milton says in the above epigraph. But his obscurity would soon disappear.

The moment of his baptism is called the Epiphany, an English translation of *epiphanaia*, which means "astonishing appearance." Jesus as the Christ, or Messiah, was revealed for the first time as he stepped from the river: "And Jesus, when he was baptized, went up immediately out of the water: and, lo, the heavens were opened unto him, and he saw the Spirit of God descending like a dove, and lighting upon him." Soon a voice came from heaven: "This is my beloved son, in whom I am well pleased" (Matthew 3:16–17). From this moment on, he's out walking in the world, healing and teaching, gathering disciples, preaching that God's kingdom was at hand—like ripe fruit on the tree of life.

An actual dove did not descend upon Jesus in any of the gospel accounts. Instead, the spirit fell upon him "like a dove," and the imagery of this graceful bird has grown familiar because of iconic paintings of this scene, such as Andrea del Verrocchio's depiction of 1475, which shows a brilliantly lit white dove appearing directly over the head of Jesus, with hands (of God?) setting it afloat while two small angels watch the baptism (at least one of these angels may have been painted by Leonardo da Vinci, a young apprentice of Verrocchio). Dove or no dove, Jesus was filled with the God's spirit, experiencing a sense of rebirth, renewal, and mission.

The notion that God should speak—becoming a Voice—is rooted in the Jewish tradition, as "it was a firmly held rabbinic conviction that saints and teachers were commended in public by a heavenly Voice," says Vermes. "Furthermore, when such a commendation is directly accredited to God, the person in whose favor it is made is alluded to as 'my son.'"[1] The next time we hear God speak from heaven about his son in these terms will be toward the end of Jesus's public ministry, on the mountain when he undergoes the change from earthly body into spiritual body known as the Transfiguration. Again, the voice proclaims a revelation.

A crucial figure in the life of Jesus is John the Baptist, his cousin, "the one who goes before him in the spirit and power of Elijah" (Luke 1:17). Scholars widely accept him as a historical person, as Josephus mentions him. A wild ascetic in the gospels, the Baptist embodies "a voice crying in the wilderness" (Mark 1:3). His appearance startled people, as he wore a crude garment made from camel's hair and refused to shave or cut his hair or make polite conversation. He was a solitary (probably an Essene at one point) who fasted and prayed for long periods (Matthew 1:18). Many thought he harbored a devil. Some theologians have argued that "John the Baptist may have been an angelic pre-existent spirit," therefore not obliged to descend into the flesh, as Rowan Williams observes.[2] Interestingly, a cult centered in Alexandria grew up around him — a movement that actually rivaled the religion of Jesus, even though he was quite explicit about his being a forerunner of the Messiah, not the Messiah himself. "He must increase, but I must decrease," said John, rather modestly, of himself in relation to Jesus. (Then again, Christian evangelists wrote the gospels.)

In Acts 18:24–25, one sees how highly John the Baptist stood in particular circles. On his travels, the apostle Paul met a man called Apollos, a native of Alexandria. He's described as "an eloquent man, well-versed in the scriptures." In a telling comment, Paul explains that Apollos had been "instructed in the Way of the Lord," and yet he knew only of John the Baptist, not Jesus. This suggests that the idea of the Way of the Lord was less tied to the person of Jesus than is often assumed. Paul notes with considerable unease in writing to the Corinthian church that people were being baptized in many names, not only in the name of Jesus. This struck him as a dangerous precedent, given that any number of wandering preachers claimed spiritual authority.

This was, as I've noted, an era rich in prophets and fiery rebels, magicians and freaks, some of them holy men in the tradition of charismatic Judaism (and with emotional ties to older prophets, such as Elijah). The practice of baptism, however, was not something original or strange among these types. In fact, ritual immersion had been a common practice among Jews throughout the Second Temple period, as scholars have observed. It was often preceded by "a time of careful teaching in the Torah and the Prophets and in the proper way to observe the traditions of Judaism."[3]

Ritual bathing remains a common practice throughout the

world: everyone has seen pictures of Hindus plunging into the
Ganges. This ritual takes on symbolic overtones when it becomes baptism, a rite of transformation. In the Christian tradition, baptism is a crucial sacrament, a sign of God's willingness
to accept a soul into the fold, and — in adult baptism — it signals
a renewal and commitment to the Way of Jesus, a life dedicated
to others, a life of worship and adherence to specific ideals. The
practice acquired a fresh intensity with John the Baptist. He
used the ritual of full immersion as a sign of spiritual awakening, as in *metanoia*, which (as explained earlier) in addition to
signaling a change of heart means to open one's mind to God
and thus be filled with new life. The person being baptized has
made a commitment to reordering priorities and seeking what
Jesus called "the kingdom of heaven." For John, in particular,
the act of baptism suggested death and rebirth through spiritual
cleansing.

In this time of intense political instability, the secular powers feared John's popularity. Herod Antipas (a son of Herod)
ruled in Perea and Galilee, where he rivaled his father in his
penchant for sheer — almost gleeful — brutality. According to
Mark (6:7–8), John disapproved of this ruler's marriage to the
wife of his half brother, Philip I; he denounced him bluntly, saying: "It is not lawful for you to possess your brother's wife." This
was too sharply critical, especially coming from one who had attracted a following of his own, and John soon found himself im-
prisoned in the frontier fortress of Machaerus, where he was beheaded at the request of Salome, the king's stepdaughter. (She
seems to have bewitched Antipas with her belly dancing — a detail that Mark could not pass over.) John's head arrived at the
palace on a silver platter, a vision that Titian painted memorably in the early sixteenth century, with the innocent face of Salome hovering near the ghastly severed head as if to say, "You
mean *I* did that?"

The Temptation in the Desert

John the Baptist fades from history, but Jesus emerges. Empowered by his baptism, with the vocal approval of God, he did as many ascetics had done before him: took himself into the desert for forty days. This was a symbolic number, paralleling both the years spent in the desert by ancient Israel on their journey to the land of Canaan and the fasting time of Moses before he received the Ten Commandments: "And he was there with the LORD forty days and forty nights; he did neither eat bread, nor drink water" (Exodus 34:28). Fasting often marks the prelude to a period of spiritual testing, which followed in the desert, when Satan appeared before Jesus with a series of tests.

In Mark, the temptation of Christ gets short shrift — almost everything gets short shrift in Mark — while in Luke and Matthew the authors expand on it vividly. How could they resist? Their accounts conform in so many ways that scholars attribute the nearly identical conversations between Jesus and the Devil to Q, a lost source that the writers of these gospels drew on for details. (Q refers to *Quelle*, a German word for "source.") The temptation scene is absent from John altogether, which (with other evidence) leads us to believe the author of the Fourth Gospel had probably not read the three so-called Synoptic Gospels (from a Greek word that means "seeing together," suggesting that Mark, Matthew, and Luke drew on the same sources, with the latter two evangelists copying from Mark, often word for word).

The larger mythic question is this: Why does the story of the ministry of Jesus begin in the desert, with temptations by Satan? Was it because this would make Jesus seem more like us? It's a fact that everyone is tempted by one thing or another. Error is sin, a stepping off the "right" or "straight" path; the word "right" in Anglo-Saxon means the direct or straight route from one point to another. The "wrong" path is the "crooked" one. As the Lord's Prayer says: "Lead us not into temptation, but deliver us from evil." Evil, again, is error, a misstep, a move in the wrong direction — *hamartia* in Greek, meaning "off the mark." We all get off the path now and then, sometimes wildly off course. I don't want to downplay here the meaning of sin, however. As William Law, an Anglican devotional writer of the eighteenth century, put it very sharply: "The whole nature of the Christian religion stands on these two great pillars, namely the greatness of our fall and the greatness of our redemption."[4]

Try to imagine Jesus, led by the Spirit, wandering in the desert, fasting and praying, feeling his own sweat and stench, the gritty sand in the folds of his skin, in his hair. Dryness would have parched his skin, a mirror of the spiritual aridity he sought to relieve through prayer and fasting. John the Baptist had lived in this manner for years, and this wasn't as odd as it sounds. Holy men often went into the desert for long spells of solitude, but Jesus did so at the age of thirty, having been perhaps a carpenter for more than a decade. Within hours, Jesus would surely have grown hungry, so it makes sense that the first temptation involved turning stones into bread. Jesus replied to Satan with consummate poise: "One does not live by bread alone" (Matthew 4:4). Here he simply quoted (indirectly) Deuteronomy 8:3: "And he humbled thee, and suffered thee to hunger, and fed thee with manna, which thou knewest not, neither did thy fathers know; that he might make thee know that man doth not live by bread only, but by every word that proceedeth out of the mouth of the Lord doth man live." That is, we live not by ingesting mere food; in fact, the material world fails to satisfy our full spiritual needs.

In the second temptation (or third one, depending on whether you follow Luke or Matthew, who reverse the order and differ on whether the temptations occurred during or after the forty days), Satan led Jesus to the top of the Temple in Jerusalem, telling him to jump off to prove that he is God's son, as God would surely supply enough angels to break his fall if he were truly divine. Jesus rightly mocked this suggestion, saying tersely: "Do not put the Lord your God to the test." The third temptation found Jesus and Satan with a commanding view from the highest mountain in the desert, from which it was possible to see "all the kingdoms of the world and their splendor" (Matthew 4:8). Satan offered this geographical expanse to Jesus if he would only worship him, not God — Satan's version of what is now often called "the prosperity gospel" by shady televangelists, who regularly manipulate their flocks by offering a path to earthly riches, as if the kingdom of God had any monetary basis. Jesus merely scoffed at Satan here, as well he should: "Get away from me!"

Matthew and Luke tell the same story in the same words, although their reversal of the order of the second and third temptation remains a point of curiosity for scholars, suggesting that authorial discretion played a role. That is, the writers of these gospels worked from oral and perhaps written traditions, picking and choosing, ordering their material in a fictive way (fiction derives from a Latin word — *fictio* — meaning to shape material, highlighting some things, suppressing others.) In each of the temptations set before him, Jesus replied to Satan in his inimical style, saying: *Don't tempt me, and don't try to put God in a position to rescue me.* In his behavior with the Adversary, he showed us exactly how to act when tempted: You sidestep the tempter, and walk away.

In *The Hero with a Thousand Faces*, Joseph Campbell has described what he calls a "monomyth," the classic journey of the hero, a story that underlies most narratives that feature a spiritual transformation. The hero — Moses, the Buddha, Jesus, Odysseus, or virtually any heroic figure — follows a familiar path: "A hero ventures forth from the world of common day into a region of supernatural wonder: fabulous forces are there encountered and a decisive victory is won: the hero comes back from this mysterious adventure with the power to bestow boons on his fellow man."[5] Soon after the hero's "call to adventure," his summons to follow a unique path occurs, and he must go into the wilderness (literally and figuratively); he must be tempted. As Campbell observes, the tests that a hero confronts often come in threes, and the story of Jesus follows the pattern. He meets three "tests" or "temptations" — the Greek word is *ekpeiraseis*, which means "a putting on trial." The point of these temptations seems clear: the humanity of Jesus requires that he, like everyone, face trials in his life, and the way forward means dealing successfully with these tests. In Hebrews 4:15, the writer — writing in the tradition of Paul's letters — suggests that in Jesus his followers possess a "high priest" who is "in every respect tested as we are."[6]

The Ministry Begins

For Jesus, this time in the desert clarified his intentions, and he resolved to take his mission into the world. But how would he do this? Where to begin? He had no formal education, no wealthy or influential family behind him. In fact, his family appears to have regarded him as somewhat volatile, even mad. One sees this in the Gospel of Mark, where the evangelist tells us that when he was preaching to a large crowd one of his family members said: "He's out of his mind" (Mark 3:21). They tried, without luck, to "take custody of him" at one point, hoping his radical energies might be restrained. It's obvious that Jesus did not have an easy time in Nazareth, among family members and neighbors who had watched him grow and wondered why he had come back from the desert full of strange ideas.

As Luke tells it, he had a rocky debut as a preacher in his home town.[7] On a fateful day, he went to the local synagogue where he must have worshipped for decades on the Sabbath. Surrounded by familiar faces, he stepped forward to read from the sacred scrolls, choosing a passage from Isaiah, a familiar text: "The Spirit of the Lord is upon me, because he has anointed me to bring good news to the poor. He has sent me to proclaim release to the captives and recovery of sight to the blind, to let the oppressed go free, to proclaim the year of the Lord's favor" (Luke 4:18–19). So far, so good. Everyone would have nodded wisely. But then Jesus said: "Today this scripture is fulfilled in your hearing" (Luke 4:21). Hearing this, the crowd grew restive, even angry. Did Jesus somehow imagine he could fulfill this prophecy in his own person? Wasn't this the carpenter's son? Perhaps he really was crazy, as some had already suggested.

That Jesus would speak at all in the synagogue suggests he must already have established himself as someone with spiritual authority and rabbinical skills, and some that day were "amazed by his gracious words." In his reading from Isaiah, it's clear that Jesus did some editing of the text, mixing passages from chapters sixty-one and fifty-eight. Kenneth E. Bailey, a biblical scholar who has spent much of his life in Israel, suggests that this community would have known this particular passage well, as it lay "at the heart of their history and self-understanding."[8] Bailey notes that in the Targumim — a first-century translation of the Hebrew Bible into Aramaic — there was an emphasis in this passage on the triumph of Jewish settlers over their gentile neighbors, who had pushed into this region of Galilee in ways that threatened Jewish settlements. In this charged atmosphere, there would have been strong resistance to the political message that Jesus seemed to repress in favor of a more spiritual one. They would have asked why he chose to turn a passage about the triumph of the Jews into one about paying attention to the poor and afflicted.

As Bailey observes, fragments from the Dead Sea Scrolls suggest that Jesus was preaching on a theme very much in the air in the early decades of the first century, especially among the Essenes, who strongly identified with the poor (being forerunners of later monastic orders, who took vows of poverty). In fact, many scholars have wondered if Jesus might actually have belonged to this sect at one point, or at least have been deeply influenced by their teachings.[9]

That Jesus identified himself as one anointed for this work of "proclamation" certainly agitated the Nazarenes. To their ears, his interpretation of a beloved passage smacked of heresy and self-delusion, and the appropriate punishment for heretics was stoning. "And they were offended by him," Luke writes. "But Jesus said to them, A prophet is not without honor except in his own country or in his own house" (Luke 13:61). At this point, Jesus had riled the crowd to such a point that they actually drove him from the synagogue to a cliff at the outskirts of the village. They intended to push him over the edge, a fall that might have resulted in death or severe injury. But for mysterious reasons they didn't.

Did Jesus say something to defuse the tension? (He was clever on his feet, capable of withering remarks, and there was also the local-boy factor. Would they really push the son of Mary and Joseph over the edge of a cliff?) One regrets that none of the gospel writers gives us more details, as the scene cries out for elaboration. All we know is that Jesus escaped the hostile intentions of his neighbors, that he walked away unharmed. Perhaps he spoke to them in his usual frank way, engaging their sympathy, reminding them of something he had said or done before. Did he call them out by name, fixing them with a familiar gaze? All of this is left, like so much in the gospels, to the imagination of readers. Positioned, as in Luke, at the outset of the ministry, this incident in the synagogue sets the scene for all the trouble that would follow, as Jesus continued to press against the boundaries of taste and received wisdom, angering many who heard him, setting the stage for his eventual arrest and execution.

The incident in the synagogue — and the reaction of the local community—frightened the family of Jesus, and their fears only intensified when he began to move from village to village, exorcizing demons and healing the sick, attracting large crowds and gossip, too. That he brazenly sought out whores and slaves, lepers and tax collectors—people on the bottom of the pecking order—didn't reassure them. Even though an angel of the Lord had prepared Mary for something unusual, her son's behavior probably confused and upset her. (Joseph may have been dead by this time, as no further mention of him will be found in the gospels or any further book of the New Testament.) Eventually, however, the family accepted Jesus as a gifted rabbi, if not the Messiah. Indeed, his brother James would actually play a large role in the early Christian communities, directing its operations from Jerusalem, rivaled only by Paul as a shaping force in the decades after their leader's departure.

And yet there is the discomforting fact that Jesus had reservations about family life, especially as it relates to discipleship. He asked his followers to reject their loved ones if they really wished to join his mission. His directives could be vehement, as in Luke 14:26: "If anyone comes to me and does not hate his father and mother, his wife and children, his brothers and sisters—yes, even his own life—he cannot be my disciple." However you examine this and other passages, it's obvious that Jesus made uncompromising demands on those who would follow him: not unlike the Therapeutae—one of several monastic sects of the era who favored living apart from family in the pursuit of spiritual goals.

His own relations with his mother often seem puzzling, as in the wedding at Cana, where he performed his first miracle. The story appears only in John 2:1–11, which presents this magical tale with a compressed grace:

> On the third day there was a wedding in Cana of Galilee, and the
> mother of Jesus was there. Jesus and his disciples had also been

invited to the wedding. When the wine ran out, the mother of
Jesus said to him, "They have no wine." And Jesus said to her,
"Woman, what concern is that to you or to me? My hour has not
yet come." His mother said to the servants, "Do whatever he tells
you." Now standing nearby were six stone water jars for the Jewish rites of purification, each holding twenty or thirty gallons. Jesus said to them, "Fill the jars with water." And they filled them
up to the brim. He then said to them, "Now draw some out, and
take it to the chief steward." So they took it. When the steward
tasted the water that had become wine, and did not know where
it came from (though the servants who had drawn the water
knew), the steward called the bridegroom and said to him, "Everyone serves the good wine first, and then the inferior wine after
the guests have become drunk. But you have kept the good wine
until now." Jesus did this, the first of his signs, in Cana of Galilee,
and revealed his glory; and his disciples believed in him.

A few things stand out in this passage. For a start, Jesus and
his disciples chose to attend this wedding with Mary, who obviously played a large role in the life of her son, or he would not
have come. For all his comments about putting aside one's family to follow him, Jesus didn't disapprove of weddings. His public ministry begins, in earnest, at such an occasion. And a wedding, then as now, was worthy of celebration, so the lack of wine
threatened to dampen the spirits of those in attendance. But
why did Mary complain about the wine to Jesus? What did she
really expect of him?

The response to Mary sounds rude to modern ears:
"Woman, what concern is that to you and to me? My hour has
not yet come." What hour did he mean? Did this ominous-
sounding phrase anticipate his death on the cross? Or did this
allude to his ministry at large, which was only just beginning?
There is no doubt, to me, that Jesus implicitly affirmed the ritual of marriage by staging his first miracle or "sign" at such an

event. This point takes on some importance in the context of Paul — a major theological force — who would later say that it was "better to marry than to burn" (I Corinthians 7:9). That's not a ringing endorsement of holy matrimony. Yet it seems important that the ministry of Jesus began where it did — at a wedding feast, with his mother in attendance.

Family life mattered to him, even though we get only brief glimpses of him in that context, creating a narrative vacuum where rumors flood in, many of them unfounded. The notion that Jesus was married seems to have traveled widely — from the Mormon preacher Orson Hyde, who argued that Jesus was a polygamist who married Mary Magdalene and Martha and perhaps another Mary, to *The Da Vinci Code*, a popular novel by Dan Brown that claimed Mary Magdalene as the wife of Jesus. No canonical details give credence to such notions, though in two of the Gnostic Gospels — *The Gospel of Mary* and *The Gospel of Philip* — one finds references to Mary Magdalene that could lead one to assume that Jesus felt especially close to her. In *Philip*, for instance, Jesus kissed Mary Magdalene on the lips. It's worth noting this, if only to remind us that the Jesus story cannot easily be confined to the handful of documents selected as canonical by bishops in later centuries. The life itself forms a wide-ranging and complex *mythos* with countless stray elements that challenge orthodox views at every turn. (The recent discovery of an ancient Coptic fragment that alludes to the wife of Jesus has created further interest in the notion that Jesus could have been married, although most scholars dismiss the idea as unlikely, given that the gospels — even those outside the canon — make no reference to any wife of Jesus, and they would probably have noted this, as they mention that others in his circle, such as Peter, had a wife. It would have been odd to leave out such a key piece of biographical information.)[10]

From Cana, Jesus set forth in earnest, speaking to large or small crowds in his unique fashion, gathering disciples, baptizing those who wished to change their lives, preaching in ways that challenged and startled those who heard him, casting out demons, healing the blind and deaf, the palsied, the leprous. He raised several people from the dead (not just Lazarus), and that wasn't the half of it. As John remarks at the end of his gospel, "There are also many other things that Jesus did; if every one of them were written down, I suppose that the world itself could not contain the books that would be written" (John 21:25). No wonder his legend spread, a stone tossed into a pond with ever-widening circles. The larger significance of the gospel story is put simply by Thomas à Kempis: "God can do more than man can understand."[11]

4

Walking in Galilee: The Healer and Teacher

Jesus said, "I am not your master. Because you
have drunk, you have become drunk from the
babbling stream which I have measured out."

— *GOSPEL OF THOMAS*

Here are your waters, and your watering place.
Drink and be whole again beyond confusion.

— ROBERT FROST, "Directive"

I still have many things to say to you,
but you cannot bear them now.

— JOHN 16:12

Watering Place

AFTER HIS HAIR-RAISING debut at the synagogue in Nazareth, Jesus set out on his public ministry in a determined fashion, walking through Galilee
and neighboring provinces. His exact travels vary in the different gospel accounts, but the general directions remain clear, extending out from Capernaum and bordering regions, ending in
Jerusalem. From the moment of his baptism, however, he un-

derstood and even embraced his fate, although its lineaments emerged gradually.

His ministry became a series of encounters, one-on-one confrontations that changed the lives of those who met him, whether they came to him for healing or instruction. Some brushed against him by accident; yet few didn't feel the force of their meeting with the Son of Man. Each felt the mystery and power of his presence, his intense contact with the kingdom of God, his emotional and intellectual resources, the life-enhancing waters that flowed from him.

One example will stand in for many. In John's gospel, he traveled widely on foot from Judea through Samaria, heading back to his base in Galilee, then heading out again. He and his disciples baptized people wherever they went, often going off in pairs to do this work at the behest of Jesus. In Samaria, in a town called Sychar, where Jacob had a well in ancient times, Jesus is seen by himself; exhausted, he sat by this particular well. It was noon when a Samaritan woman stopped to draw water.

"Will you give me a drink?" Jesus asked.[1]

It shocked her that he spoke to her at all, let alone with a request like this one. "You're a Jew," she said. "I'm a Samaritan woman. And you ask me for a drink!"

Jews and Samaritans did not associate in those times, and — probably more to the point — a self-respecting Jewish man did not speak to a strange woman at a public place like a well. But Jesus would speak to anyone, wherever and whenever he chose.

The conversation turned progressively more complex, testier, with the stakes increasing as they spoke.[2]

He said to her: "If you had any idea who asked you for a drink, and what God can do actually for you, you would have asked if this man could give you some living water."

She replied: "Sir, you have nothing to use to draw water, no bucket. This well is very deep. And where can one get this living water you talk about? Don't tell me you're more important than Jacob, our father, who gave us this well and drank from it himself, as have his sons and their animals for generations."

Jesus said, "Those who drink this water will grow thirsty again. But whoever drinks the water I offer won't thirst again. I provide the waters of eternal life."

She smiled, wise-cracking. "Please give me this amazing water, so I won't get thirsty again, and I won't have to keep coming here to draw water."

Jesus had her number, however. "Go get your husband. Tell him to come here."

"I have no husband," she replied coolly.

"That's true," said Jesus. "In fact, you've had five husbands, and the man you're living with at the moment isn't even your husband."

Now she was flummoxed, even frightened. How did he know all of this? "Sir, you're a prophet. I see that now."

They talked more, and the wheels in her head began to spin. She said, "I know that the Messiah is coming. When he comes, he'll explain everything to us."

He responded, "I, the one speaking to you, am he."

Shocked by this statement, and convinced of its truth, she rushed to tell people in the village about the compelling if rather testy man she had just met at Jacob's Well.

Like so many of the encounters between Jesus and a stranger, this anecdote layers meaning on meaning. Jesus had been walking for a long time and was "weary" (Greek: *kopiao*, meaning "beaten down"). In his exhaustion, he stands in for each of us, travelers who stop for refreshment at the hottest time of the day without a bucket but thirsty. In the midst of this crisis comes an opportunity, which is always for Jesus a moment of human exchange and transformation. (He is transformed as much as the person encountered, as he grows into his prophetic role, testing the limits of his own gifts.)

This time, he encounters a double alien: a woman and a Samaritan. Self-respecting men didn't talk to strange women, especially in these circumstances. But Jesus felt her yearning, her fragility masked by bravado. He always broke down barriers, never erected them. The fact that she was a Samaritan, with "heretical" views, didn't faze him. As a race, the Samaritans mingled Jewish and Assyrian ancestry, blending so-called heathen practices with traditional Jewish worship. Josephus in his *Antiquities* calls them "idolaters and hypocrites," and this view prevailed within orthodox Jewish circles. So Jesus took a risk in speaking with this woman, inviting her to give him a drink.

As ever, Jesus spoke in metaphors, indirectly. The literal image quickly became a symbol here: real water transformed into "living water," water from a spiritual wellspring. What Jesus offered was a fresh way of looking at the world, a new code of behavior. You talked to women without troubling over gender rules. You confronted people about their past lives, their current situation. You didn't worry about their racial or political origins but sought to bring them into a state of reconciliation with God, a condition of atonement that would fill them with "living water" that reached beyond physical thirst. Hardly any story in the gospels seems more to the point, more instructive, on such different levels.

Going Out from Capernaum

At the start of his ministry, Jesus established a base of operations at the northwestern end of the Sea of Galilee, at Capernaum — a village directly on the Silk Road that marked the last stretch of territory ruled by Herod Antipas. Lower Galilee (the Hebrew word means "circle" or "district") was known for its great physical beauty: forests and fertile land, the lake itself, and the smooth shoulders of green hills. Light breezes carried whiffs of lavender and thyme to nearby villages. Sheep and cattle grazed in valleys. It was a bountiful place, as Josephus notes, saying that Galilee was "rich in soil and pasturage" and possessed such a "variety of trees" that most residents devoted themselves to agriculture, the easiest way to earn a living there. A distinction should be made, however: Upper Galilee was almost a separate country: hilly, remote, overrun by bandits and political or religious zealots. Lower Galilee, on the other hand, was fertile, abundant. Villages dotted the lower region, which bordered the Sea of Galilee on the east, with the Mediterranean (near what is now Haifa) on the west. It was in this region that Jesus focused his ministry.

The major cities of Sepphoris and Tiberias lay at the southern end of Galilee, and these attracted traders from far and wide. But in the course of his ministry, Jesus seems to have skirted them, preferring a rural ministry and village life.

In Capernaum, Jesus began to gather disciples, enlisting four sturdy fishermen almost at once: Simon (Peter), Andrew, James, and John. (The latter may have been the so-called Beloved Disciple, a mysterious figure mentioned in the gospels but without citing his actual name.) Within a short time he added Philip, Matthew, Nathanael (also called Bartholomew), Thomas, James, Simon the Zealot, Judas (also called Thaddaeus), and Judas Iscariot — twelve in all, in symbolic conjunction with the twelve tribes of Israel. The names vary slightly as they appear in the gospels and this confuses readers. Peter, for instance, was also called Simon — a fairly common Hebrew name. Jesus sometimes referred to him as Kephas, in Aramaic, adding to the confusion. In Greek, his name was Petros (meaning "rock"). Peter — on whom Jesus by tradition had built his church — was a married man. (We know this because he had a mother-in-law whom Jesus healed when he found her in bed with a fever.) Probably most of the disciples lived in or around Capernaum, and one can only imagine what private dramas may have taken place within their households as they tried to explain to their families that they planned to drop everything and follow Jesus.

Mary Magdalene entered the picture early. She was not among the twelve disciples but played a huge role in his ministry; she was there at the foot of the cross and was, crucially, the first person to see him after his resurrection, as recorded in both Mark and John. She was (by tradition) the author of the apocryphal *Gospel of Mary*, discovered in 1896 but probably dating from the second century. One should also note a line from the *Pistis Sophia* — a significant Gnostic text also dating from the second century — where Jesus says that Mary Magdalene would "tower over all my disciples." That Jesus enormously valued her company cannot be doubted, though the idea that Mary Magdalene was more than a very dear friend remains a point of speculation.

Although unmarried, Jesus liked being around women, and made a point of including them in his company. A good picture of what his ministry looked like appears in Luke 8:1–3: "Soon afterwards he went on through cities and villages, proclaiming and bringing the good news of the kingdom of God. The twelve were with him, as well as some women who had been cured of evil spirits and infirmities: Mary, called Magdalene, from whom seven demons had been cast out, and Joanna, the wife of Herod's steward Chuza, and Susanna, and many others." Women followed him eagerly, and many became leaders in the early Christian church. It was much later — many decades after his death — that misogyny took root in the church, making it awkward for women to assume leadership roles. But Jesus himself never shied away from women, nor did he discourage them from assuming spiritual authority in his name.

The twelve disciples remain fairly indistinct, though we pick up tidbits of individuality here and there. There were two pairs of brothers: Peter and Andrew, James and John. Philip was born in Bethsaida, the home of Andrew and Peter, and he appears to have spoken Greek (instead of Aramaic), so he later traveled to Greece, Phrygia, and Syria to convert the gentiles in their familiar tongue. Simon the Zealot was sometimes called Simon the Cananaean (or Canaanite), and one assumes he had strong political views, given his membership in the revolutionary Zealots. His presence reminds us that, however spiritual the kingdom of God might be, there was a political element in play, and Jesus acknowledged this by including Simon among his twelve. On quite another note, Matthew was a tax collector — a disreputable occupation among Jews, who loathed the Roman authorities — and he may be the one called Levi in Mark. By allowing a tax collector among his closest followers, Jesus showed everyone he met that he took no obvious political side in the struggles between Roman rule and its client kings in Palestine. Thaddaeus was also called Judas, but he was *not* the Judas who betrayed Jesus in the final days. That was Judas Iscariot — a creature of legend, much of it post-biblical. We learn in Acts 1:26 that to replace Judas, "the lot fell upon Matthias." This way, the number could remain twelve. But Matthias remains a bit of a mystery, lost in the pages of history.

Modern archaeologists have added a good deal to our sense of the historical reality behind the ministry of Jesus. They found, for instance, the remains of an ancient synagogue in Capernaum — possibly the exact spot where Jesus taught. When he took up preaching there, the people listened keenly and "were astounded by his teaching, because his words had authority" (Luke 4:32). He taught them that the kingdom of God lay at hand, even within them, and urged them to open their hearts and minds to the spiritual realities he had himself experienced, inviting them to drink from the living waters.

One of his earliest acts — a public demonstration of his unusual gifts — was to cast out a demon from a severely deranged man, an exorcism that startled the village where the man had lived. Later, he cured Peter's mother-in-law of a fever, and news spread quickly about this wonder-working healer who had fetched up in Capernaum to perform amazing feats. Crowds gathered at sunset outside of Peter's house, where those with "various kinds of sickness" surrounded Jesus, who healed them one by one, ever patient, always listening as much as speaking.

Jesus also spent time instructing the twelve in Capernaum, making sure they understood his ideas before they took his ministry on the road. At one point, he gathered a child into his arms and declared: "Whoever receives one child in my name receives me." The message came through loudly: *Don't let your ego get in the way of your goal, which is to spread the good news of the kingdom. And remember that it's not a complicated message, as any child can receive it. Go with your heart, not your head.*

The story of Jesus as healer and exorcist has a peculiar ring today. But in Palestine twenty centuries ago, healers and exorcists roamed the landscape, many of them quite gifted. In truth, nobody in the gospels seems to have doubted that Jesus performed miracles of healing or cast out demons; it was only a question of *in whose name* he performed these mighty acts.[3] To me, it's not surprising in the least that Jesus could empower those with physical ailments or "demons" to recover: faith is a tonic, and Jesus asked those he healed to put their trust *not in himself but in God.*

Great men in the ancient world were often thought to perform miracles. Philo, a major Jewish writer and contemporary of Jesus, writes that the Emperor Augustus was an "averter of evil" who quieted storms and stopped plagues, and nobody questioned this assumption. People thought that the Emperor Nero had quelled a storm, too.[4] Indeed, the kinds of miracles that Jesus performed suited an age before the advent of psychoanalysis or antidepressants. He had a surprising talent for opening up the victims of madness to healing energies, and this doesn't sound especially "supernatural" to me. It may require a stretch to imagine he could make a blind man see or a victim of paralysis walk; but I have no doubt that faith can boost one's immune system and that its emotional balm has healing effects. Most of the other miracles in the gospels, such as walking on water or quelling storms or turning water into wine, strike me as intensely symbolic acts and should be considered as such. This doesn't mean they should not be considered true as well. It means that the writers of the gospels had a different view of truth from that held by modern philosophers and historians who, in Oscar Wilde's sublime phrase, are "always degrading truths into facts."[5]

The gospels offer tantalizing glimpses of the public ministry of Jesus, repeating things he said in slightly altered form — not a surprising thing, given that Matthew and Luke appropriated much of Mark. Plagiarism was not a problem in those days, and one assumes in any case that Jesus repeated himself: all teachers do. He honed his message on the stump, finding the right emphases, the best rhetorical structures for making his points. This must have been a superb time for him and his disciples, who reveled in his presence, consumed by his fiery nature, his wit and wisdom, his superb knowledge of Hebrew scripture, his sense of God's presence working in his life and potentially transforming theirs as well as they shifted from village to village, often sleeping outside under the stars, bypassing towns and cities by going through the countryside, where they slept in fields or barns. Needless to say, both the Roman and Jewish authorities looked warily on this itinerant band, who seemed oblivious at times to laws and customs.

One gets a hint of the immediate problem in Mark 2:23–28, where Jesus and his followers "went through the fields of grain" near a village "on the Sabbath day." As they walked, the disciples of Jesus blithely plucked "corn" (probably barley) at random. This annoyed the local Pharisees, who followed Sabbath laws with fanatical rigidity, assuming that the way into God's kingdom involved adherence to specific codes. You simply didn't reap on the Sabbath, even if you needed food. The Pharisees—as strict followers of Mosaic law—complained to Jesus, who explained that King David himself had gone into the high priest's house once and taken the "show bread," which only priests could eat with impunity; he gave this bread to his hungry followers. And why not? David was a king, after all, and it was good to be king.

Jesus's lackadaisical response to Jewish law shocked and annoyed the Pharisees. Who did he think he was? Was this young man from a poor family in Nazareth claiming to be a royal personage, even David reborn? Did he have any idea how scandalous he sounded? Jesus listened to them respectfully but rebuffed their legalistic thinking: "The Sabbath was made for man, and not man for the Sabbath: Therefore the Son of Man should also be considered Lord also of the Sabbath."[6] One can only imagine their response.

One tracks Jesus in his daily ministry in different ways in the four gospels, and it's impossible to get a clear route or sense of chronology. Yet a kind of summary of his work appears in Matthew 4:23–25: "And Jesus walked about Galilee, teaching in the synagogues, preaching the gospel of the kingdom, and healing every kind of sickness and disease among the people. And his fame spread even throughout Syria: and they brought unto him sick people that were taken with different illnesses and torments, and those who were possessed with devils, and those that were mad, and those that had forms of paralysis and palsy; and he healed them. And vast multitudes followed him from Galilee, and from Decapolis, and from Jerusalem, and from Judaea, and from beyond the Jordan." Although glimpses of him occur in various parts of Palestine, he confined himself to Galilee and its shorelines for the most part, with a final journey to Jerusalem through Judea and Perea.

The exact length of his ministry remains unknown, though he apparently began preaching and teaching when he was "about thirty years old" (Luke 3:23). The events described in Mark could easily have taken place within a single year or less, even a few months, and this is true of Matthew and Luke as well. Only one Passover celebration is mentioned in the Synoptic Gospels, hence the assumption that the ministry occupied him for a year or so. In John, however, three Passovers occurred in the course of the public ministry, which suggests to many readers that three years must have elapsed. But the gospels' narratives follow no timeline, and events in the story occur in a different order in each version, and the lapse of time is impossible to gauge. Not being biography in the modern sense of that term, the gospels should be taken as impressionistic accounts of an extraordinary life, and the authors (probably many authors, who expanded and modified earlier texts) shift the scene of the action from one place to another almost at will to illustrate the sort of things that Jesus did, often gathering the specific teachings of Jesus into neat summaries — not unlike the helter-skelter way in which they would have been presented in real time.

Matthew, in particular, arranged the teachings in well-defined sections. This gospel may actually have been a textbook, written in Antioch for an audience of students at what might have been a very early Christian seminary of sorts.[7] It puts forward a tidy compilation of sayings and parables, laid out in didactic fashion. At the core of this teaching lies the Sermon on the Mount, which draws on vast reservoirs of desert wisdom, looking to the East as well as the West for inspiration and ideas. If it were the only record of Jesus that survived, it would suffice to place him among the handful of major spiritual and ethical guides in history.

The Sermon on the Mount

The Sermon on the Mount begins with a series of statements known as the Beatitudes (Matthew 5:3–12). These aphorisms reach far beyond the ethics of traditional Judaism, appropriating a version of the Hindu and Buddhist idea of Karma, which suggests that what happens to us is rooted in our deeds: If we show mercy, we receive mercy, for instance; if we behave violently, violence will define us. This is called the Karmic cycle, and it became a pervasive and grounding concept in Eastern religions. Of course, Jesus framed the concept in ways unique to himself and developed in later Christian doctrine, as in Galatians 6:7: "Whatever a man sows, that shall he reap."

The Beatitudes follow in the King James Version, as the text is so familiar:

> *Blessed are the poor in spirit: for theirs is the kingdom of heaven.*
> *Blessed are they that mourn: for they shall be comforted.*
> *Blessed are the meek: for they shall inherit the earth.*
> *Blessed are they which do hunger and thirst after righteousness: for they shall be filled.*
> *Blessed are the merciful: for they shall obtain mercy.*
> *Blessed are the pure in heart: for they shall see God.*
> *Blessed are the peacemakers: for they shall be called the children of God.*
> *Blessed are they which are persecuted for righteousness' sake: for theirs is the kingdom of heaven.*
> *Blessed are ye, when men shall revile you, and persecute you, and shall say all manner of evil against you falsely, for my sake.*
> *Rejoice, and be exceeding glad: for great is your reward in heaven: for so persecuted they the prophets which were before you.*

It was Pope Benedict XVI who said in his excellent study of the life of Jesus that anyone who reads the Sermon on the Mount attentively must realize that the Beatitudes present "a sort of veiled interior biography of Jesus, a kind of portrait of his figure."[8] We can deduce what kind of man he was from things he advocated in this sequence of statements centered on his dream of a fully realized kingdom. Each of the Beatitudes refers to this kingdom, which is already within reach of those who listen. That Jesus should begin with the "poor in spirit" matters hugely, and it embodies the most radical turn in his teaching.

Reading the Beatitudes

"Blessed are the poor in spirit." It's an appealing start, but who exactly are "the poor in spirit," and how do they relate to the poor in the usual sense, those without worldly goods? (In Luke, the opening Beatitude omits "in spirit," confusing the matter and opening a good deal of debate.) Jesus refers to an understanding of the poor as pictured in Isaiah, where "poor" refers to those with a humble demeanor. He praises this humility, which may connect to physical poverty (as it clearly does in Isaiah 58:7, where the poor are those without bread), or those requiring sustenance for their spirits. The message here seems broader, however: the humble will be blessed (Greek: *makarios*, usually translated as "blessed," also means "joyful" as well as "favored" or "happy"), and they will come into a kingdom that exists beyond time and space.

As the poor in spirit often dwelled in material poverty, the correlation between those literally and figuratively poor would not have been lost on those who listened to Jesus. The people of Palestine were hardly wealthy, and the crowds who gathered before Jesus experienced rural poverty of a grueling sort, threatened each day by hunger and disease, discouragement and fear of violence. That Jesus should speak to them, especially in the first of his Beatitudes, must have been heartening. They had a special place in God's kingdom.

There's an old Jewish story that goes like this: A rabbi is

asked why nobody sees the face of God anymore, as they did in ancient times. The rabbi says ruefully that it's because nobody these days can stoop so low.[9] In many ways this is what Jesus means in this first Beatitude: *Stoop! Find your blessings in those who lack power, wealth, or resources. Prefer humility to arrogance. This is the way to happiness, to a blessed state.*[10]

"Blessed are they that mourn." Jesus understood that life is suffering — one of the four "Noble Truths" espoused by the Buddha.[11] Jesus singles out those in special anguish, such as those who mourn the death of a loved one, the anguish of a relative or friend, the pain of illness or mental despair. For anyone, it's only a matter of time before anguish descends. As the poet Robert Hass has written: "All the new thinking is about loss." But so is all the ancient thinking. As this Beatitude suggests, in the midst of losses, God offers comfort. In fact, in times of great personal difficulty, spiritual progress becomes possible. Ever conscious of the Jewish scriptures, Jesus recalls here Ecclesiastes 7:3, where we read: "Sorrow is better than laughter: for by the sadness of the countenance the heart is made better."

"Blessed are the meek." Who are these people, the meek, who will "inherit the earth," which is quite a grand reward for their behavior? We don't usually like the meek, and the word in English has unpleasant connotations: the meek are timid, frightened, even foolish. They tug their forelocks and bow to those who are stronger. But this isn't what the Greek word (*praÿis*) actually suggests. Aristotle uses this word to mean somebody who understands the golden mean, who picks a way between anger on the one hand and subservience on the other.[12] Another translation of the Greek word is "nonviolent" or "peaceful." Further, the term correlates to a word associated in Hebrew scripture with Moses: "Now the man Moses was very meek, above all the men which were upon the face of the earth" (Numbers 12:3). One doesn't usually think of Moses, a great Israelite leader, as "meek." But the word obviously has many levels of association.

In this Beatitude, Jesus alludes specifically to a famous Hebrew text, Psalm 37:11, which reads: "But the meek shall inherit the earth; and shall delight themselves in the abundance of peace" (KJV). Those who will inherit the earth will not be aggressive or self-aggrandizing. They will be "meek," in the fullest sense of that term, nourished through its Hebrew and Greek roots.

"Blessed are they which do hunger and thirst after righteousness." The message turns on two verbs: to hunger and to thirst, words that in the context of Middle Eastern life in the first century must have carried a special vividness. Here physical needs stand in for spiritual realities. The blessed ones reach for *dikaiosuné* or "righteousness," for a condition that, in Greek, suggests a yearning for oneness with God, a conjunction of wills. "It does not mean the ethical quality of a person," cautions Bultmann. "It does not mean any quality at all, but a relationship."[13] The relationship in question is between God and the seeker, and it has to do with the seeker's actions as well, in which he or she aspires to accept and understand the will of God. And Jesus would have had in mind a passage from Isaiah 32:17: "And the work of righteousness shall be peace; and the effect of righteousness quietness and assurance forever" (KJV). The righteous shall "be filled," their hunger and thirst "satisfied" as they come into the kingdom of God.

"Blessed are the merciful." Here is an obvious reference to the Karmic cycle, as noted above. And Jesus himself showed mercy repeatedly as he moved from village to village, as when he met a blind beggar by the road (Luke 18:38) and the beggar called to him: "Jesus, son of David, have mercy on me." Jesus restored his sight at once. This willingness to act, to respond to those who ask for help, occupies the core of Christian ethics. It can't be overstated: the essential Christian urge is toward forgiveness. It should displace feelings of anger, hate, resentment, and revenge. This is a transformation that, in my view, occurs naturally as one takes up the cross of Jesus and follows him.

There is no time for revenge. One looks around and sees everywhere such need, and resolves to act, in political ways or simply personal ways, offering help to those who require counsel, friendship, food, or shelter. The natural consequence of such "mercy," of course, is forgiveness, the ultimate gift of the spirit, as it provides a conduit to atonement or union with God.

"Blessed are the pure in heart." Purity of heart belongs to those who behave without mixed motives, who live in accord with God's will, and who therefore apprehend this purity Jesus asks for. The point is amplified memorably in Titus 1:15: "To the pure all things are pure: but to those who are defiled and unbelieving, nothing is pure; even their minds and conscience are defiled." This Beatitude follows naturally from being humble and "meek," from giving to others, from listening to Jesus when he tells us to "love one another" as he loved us. But it suggests as well that the very act of striving for purity activates a vision of God: in becoming pure, we become Godlike, merging with the Spirit. We "seek his face," as Psalm 105 urges us to do, and we find it: the face of God that, as St. Augustine once suggested, we discover in the human visage of Jesus.

"Blessed are the peacemakers." Jesus blesses those who promote peace among their friends and neighbors, saying they will become the "children of God." And by extension, he blesses those who promote peace at large. These are the happy ones, the true inheritors of the kingdom; being filled with peace, they spread peacefulness around them. The peacemakers must always step forward, urging caution in situations where war or conflict arises. In an age dominated by horrendous violence and wars, these words by Jesus must have sounded a loud gong. Again, a Karmic truth emerges in this Beatitude: making peace leads to peacefulness, which ultimately defines the kingdom of God as a state of true reconciliation with the Creator. The true children of God understand that their peacefulness is a gift to the world at large.

"Blessed are they which are persecuted for righteousness' sake." This final Beatitude would have pricked the ears of his disciples, each of whom would suffer martyrdom by the end of his life. The evangelist here, writing in a time of political stress for Jews after the fall of the Second Temple in 70 CE, would also have caught the attention of severely persecuted and threatened Christians.[14] His promise to them was the ultimate boon: the kingdom of heaven, in all its dimensions, implying a kind of restoration as alienated human beings unite with the ground of their being, no longer "outside" of eternity but satisfied, complete, entering a "world without end," as we read in Ephesians 3:21. As always, righteousness means rightness with God, oneness, a convergence of the human and divine will, as seen fully within the person of Jesus himself.

Reading the Antitheses

The Beatitudes form only the first part of the Sermon on the Mount, which occupies three long chapters in Matthew. What follows directly is often called the Antitheses — six statements that adhere to a rhetorical form that would have sounded familiar to readers schooled in classical rhetoric: "You have heard it said that . . . but I tell you this." They amplify Mosaic laws in significant ways. I paraphrase them in what follows, with a brief comment on each:

1. You have heard it said, *Do not kill.* I say this: *Don't even be angry.*

    Jesus lost his temper at times, so one may well ask if he was hypocritical. On this, he might have agreed with Ralph Waldo Emerson, who said: "A foolish consistency is the hobgoblin of little minds." Jesus had a large mind and heart, and he entertained many weathers of feeling — like any human being. Yet he clearly hated injustice, poverty, and cruelty of any kind. He also understood that anger isn't a useful response, as it will eat away at the soul. Again, the idea of Karma presides, however Christianized by Jesus: anger leads to murderous behavior. Forgiveness leads to godly behavior. So he takes his listeners back to the origins of murder, anger itself.

2. You have heard it said, *Don't commit adultery.* I will go further: *Don't even lust after someone in your heart.*

   The strictness here seems, in today's erotically-charged world, to pose an impossible ideal. How can one possibly not lust after somebody in one's heart? Do we control this? Jesus was of his time, and this ideal may seem far too much to ask. But it underscores a message that still has relevance. Our lives are happier without insane lust, as Shakespeare suggests in Sonnet 129, where he writes, "The expense of spirit in a waste of shame / Is lust in action." Shakespeare meditates on lust in its various forms: past, present, and future. In each case, it roils the human spirit, producing shame, unease, blame, and myriad other distresses. It rarely helps in the pursuit of fidelity, which is where (in the Christian view) happiness lies. As Wendell Berry, the poet, has said: "What marriage offers — and what fidelity is meant to protect — is the possibility of moments when what we have chosen and what we desire are the same."[15] Jesus locates the Karmic origins of adultery in lust. It's a cycle that can only be broken at the beginning. That might seem like an impossible task; but the beginning is always coming around again, so hope lies there.

3. You have heard it said, *If you wish to divorce your wife, serve her divorce papers.* I say this: *The only way you can leave your wife is if she is unfaithful.*

   The message is clear: fidelity lies at the heart of love.

You can leave someone only if he or she has already left you. And yet Jesus builds here on the previous antithesis, where he suggests (to me) that fidelity lies at the heart of both marriage and community. And only within a community of faithful people is one actually free. Sexuality is sacramental, and when taken out of this context, it leads to exploitation. Respect, sexual discipline, and fidelity lead to the practice of love, and this is something worth practicing. And yet, as Wendell Berry further writes, "the idea of fidelity is perverted beyond redemption by understanding it as a grim, literal duty enforced only by willpower."[16] It's not about forcing the issue, settling into a joyless relationship. Fidelity and love move into the same space naturally, blossoming in the good soil of a respectful relationship.

4. You have heard it said, *Don't break an oath.* I tell you this: *Don't make promises or oaths in the first place if you're in danger of breaking them. Say yes or no, and don't hedge.*

Whatever you say, you should mean it. Be clear. Jesus calls for sincerity and transparency in making promises or commitments to others. Here he asks for fidelity of the tongue as well as the body and soul. Again, faithful speech leads to good faith. Our words must become deeds. (John P. Meier, in a long chapter on what is called the "prohibition of oaths" in the fourth volume of *A Marginal Jew*, makes the sensible point that the more severe teachings of Jesus — that one should not make oaths or promises, that one should not divorce one's spouse — are further examples of Jesus as "the eschatological prophet proclaiming the rules of conduct binding on those who already live" inside the kingdom of God.[17])

5. You have heard it said, *An eye for an eye, a tooth for a tooth.* But I tell you this: *If somebody strikes you, turn the other*

cheek. If someone demands your jacket, give it to him and your cloak as well.

This remains a core teaching of Jesus and, perhaps, his most radical revision of Judaic morality, upturning the apple cart. *Resist evil but do so without violence* is a strong message, one that influenced Tolstoy, Gandhi, and Martin Luther King. But it's a complicated matter, one that has vexed Christians throughout modern history. Political leaders who supposedly follow the Way of Jesus have rarely taken his teachings on the matter of passive resistance to evil with anything like the seriousness they require. Jesus's approach sounds too radical, a bit frightening. As human beings, our natural tendency is to strike back in self-defense if not anger. Jesus cuts against the grain, as ever, asking us to respond to evil not passively but actively, showering love and good will on those who hate us, who do us harm. He asks for restraint and much more. He asks for insane generosity: give it away, especially if you love it. Cast your bread upon the waters.

6. You have heard it said, *Love your friends but hate your enemies.* But I say this: *Love your enemies. Do good to those who try to harm you.*

This behavior represents an extension of the previous antitheses. It's an ideal, and it suggests another way to break the Karmic cycle of hatred by allowing love to flow toward even those who fall into the category of "enemies." In a sense, this love — modeled by Jesus in his life and deeds, especially in going to the cross — dissolves hatred. It's a potent instrument that makes change possible. As before, Jesus builds idea on idea, amplifying and extending his thoughts. It seems unnatural to do good to those who try to harm us; but it's the Christian way, offering an alternative to the violent response that often comes more naturally when we feel attacked.

These six antitheses take seriously the command to love. In various ways Jesus suggests that we can break cycles of violence and hatred, that the possibility of change lies before us, within our grasp. He takes every consequence back to the actions that produced it, for either good or evil, urging us to undergo a change of heart. Yet he understood that we can't simply do this hard work of transformation by ourselves. Change requires God's intervention in our lives, an overflowing of the Spirit into human consciousness. Only by the grace of God can we begin to effect change, to participate in the gradually realizing kingdom that lies within us, however difficult of access. This is not a matter of willing ourselves to perfection; it's about letting the will of God enter our lives, so that his will becomes ours: a very different dynamic.

Aware that we must seek God's help in our shift of consciousness, Jesus offered an example of prayer, a bid for grace that he asked his disciples to emulate, making prayer and meditation a central part of their spiritual practice.

The Lord's Prayer

The Lord's Prayer occupies a central place in the Sermon on the Mount, as it should. It invites us to acknowledge our imperfections, our helplessness, framing a wish for the kingdom of God to come as quickly as possible.

With a single gesture, Jesus put prayer at the center of the Christian life, and some of the most vivid scenes in the gospels occur when Jesus goes off by himself to pray, as he does in the desert or, during his final week, in the Garden of Gethsemane. Prayer was, for him, a way of opening himself to God-consciousness. It was, as prayer must be, a way of listening, allowing a kind of holy silence to fill the mind's honeycomb. A prayer is a bid (the Anglo-Saxon word for prayer is *bed*, and the Ger-

man word is *beten*; in Dutch, *bidden*), a bid for grace, for communication with the Spirit, an invitation to be filled with God's
love. We speak to God in prayer as well as listen; but we require
words, as Jesus knew, which is why he put forward this example
in Matthew 6:9–14[18]:

> *Our father, which art in heaven,*
> *Hallowed be thy name.*
> *Thy kingdom come,*
> *Thy will be done in earth,*
> *As it is in heaven.*
> *Give us this day our daily bread.*
> *And forgive us our trespasses,*
> *As we forgive them that trespass against us.*
> *And lead us not into temptation,*
> *But deliver us from evil.*
> *For thine is the kingdom,*
> *The power, and the glory,*
> *For ever and ever.*

Two versions of this prayer exist, in Matthew and Luke, and
not all manuscripts of Matthew add the doxology (the last three
lines).[19] But the character of the prayer is consistent in both versions. One begins by praising God, regarding him as a father — a
traditional Jewish idea, as when God speaks in Exodus 4:22: "Israel is my son, even my firstborn." But Jesus urged us to make
a personal connection with God, as in a father-child relationship. Every phrase in the Lord's Prayer resonates with the Jewish
scriptures, emerging from earlier concepts but always expanding, modifying, shifting as Jesus offered his followers a New
Covenant.[20]

The other elements of the prayer fall easily into place. We
invite God's kingdom to arrive sooner rather than later. God's

will (not ours) controls our aspirations, so it's no use forcing the matter, trying to grit our teeth and white-knuckle our way to perfection. We ask for "daily bread"[21] — referring here to spiritual sustenance as well as food. In keeping with what was already put forward in the Beatitudes and Antitheses, Jesus suggests that we must forgive those who do us ill while asking forgiveness for our own foolish, ill-considered, cruel, selfish, and thoughtless deeds. Penitence lies at the heart of this prayer. We must ask for forgiveness, as we inevitably fall into error, stepping off the path. We wish to be delivered from evil (in Greek, the evil one: *ho poneros* — a version of the Hebrew *Ha-satan*). Evil is everywhere around us, and we hope that God will keep us from its path. The doxology in the last three lines offers more praise to God. So the prayer begins and ends with praise. It's a wonderfully focused petition, a way to share in the prayer life of Jesus by following his example.

The immediate focus of "Thy kingdom come" — on the emerging kingdom of God — needs elaboration. The problem of exactly *when* Jesus thought the kingdom would arrive or what form it might take has vexed New Testament scholars, especially after Johannes Weiss (1863–1914), a major German theologian, put forward his theory of Jesus as a prophet obsessed with the idea of the coming "end times" or *eschaton*. And the Book of Revelation — as a conclusion to the New Testament — has not helped matters, offering a fevered vision of the final days, though it almost certainly refers to things happening at the time it was composed, not a vision of some dire end-of-the-world scenario, as Elaine Pagels has argued.[22] Indeed, it might better have been called *Apocalypse Now*.

The Lord's Prayer is gentler than anything in the Book of Revelation. It encourages a penitential attitude, so that the full benefits of prayer (which include reconciliation with God) can be experienced. This bid for grace is easily repeatable, like a mantra — as when Christians "pray the Rosary," moving from bead to bead on a necklace—where it often forms a part of a spiritual exercise.[23] This is the only time in the New Testament where we get any sense of how Jesus actually *sounded* when he prayed, and we put ourselves in his shoes by repeating these words, which engender strong emotions and open the heart to divine consciousness. We become, in the course of saying the Lord's Prayer, like Jesus himself.

Consider the Lilies

While the Lord's Prayer occupies the center of the Sermon on the Mount, Jesus follows it with a number of important sayings and exhortations as well as parables. The sixth chapter of Matthew moves toward a lovely passage, beautifully rendered by the King James translators:

> Therefore I say unto you, Take no thought for your life, what ye shall eat, or what ye shall drink; nor yet for your body, what ye shall put on. Is not the life more than meat, and the body than raiment? Behold the fowls of the air: for they sow not, neither do they reap, nor gather into barns; yet your heavenly Father feedeth them. Are ye not much better than they? Which of you by taking thought can add one cubit unto his stature? And why take ye thought for raiment? Consider the lilies of the field, how they grow; they toil not, neither do they spin: And yet I say unto you, That even Solomon in all his glory was not arrayed like one of these.

As an antidote to worry, Jesus suggested that we "consider the lilies." Faith bestows ease, confidence, and emotional balance. And here lies the reward of following the Way of Jesus: we can't add anything to our stature that God hasn't already given, by his grace. To a degree, this teaching of Jesus once again parallels a key Buddhist idea, that the universe will take care of us.

We have only to observe the present world, pay full attention to its details, and its meanings will reveal themselves: "For the heavens declare the glory of God" (Psalm 19:1).

The Golden Rule

A diamond glitters in Matthew 7:12: "Therefore all things whatsoever ye would that men should do to you, do ye even so to them: for this is the law and the prophets" (KJV). Since the Middle Ages, this piece of ancient wisdom has been called the Golden Rule.[24] It's also known, less poetically, as the ethic of reciprocity, and versions of this idea occur in most world religions, including Hinduism and Buddhism. In the *Analects* of Confucius (XV.24) another framing of this thought appears: "Do not impose on others what you yourself do not desire."[25] Similar statements go back as far as the *Code of Hammurabi* — probably the oldest written statement of this principle, dating from around 1780 BCE.[26] A version also appears in the sayings of Rabbi Hillel, a major religious leader at the time of Jesus, who delivered what is often called the Silver Rule. Hillel asks people to refrain from doing anything to others that would feel distasteful to them personally. Jesus could easily have heard this teaching from Hillel or his followers. He might have picked up versions of this idea as he talked with merchants or travelers on the Silk Road in his youth. In any case, it doesn't matter where Jesus got the idea: it was already in the air. And he improved upon it, making it central to his teaching.

Final Wisdom in the Sermon

The Sermon on the Mount ends with a blizzard of aphorisms that act as a summary of the whole, as in the following selection (KJV):

Judge not, that ye be not judged.

Ask, and it shall be given you; seek, and ye shall find.

Ye shall know them by their fruits.

It's worth recalling that aphorisms or sayings are not parables, which remain central to both the content and form of
Christian teaching. A parable is a brief, indirect story with a
moral; it may, like a Zen *koan*, provide a puzzle that needs solv-
ing — or have a point that sneaks up on the listener. The Sermon
ends with a good example of the form, the parable of the two
houses, which instructs the reader on how to interpret and *use*
the sayings of Jesus:

> Therefore whoever hears these sayings of mine, and obeys them,
> I consider him a wise man who built his house upon a rock: And
> the rain came down, and the floods came, and the winds blew,
> and beat upon that house; and yet it didn't fall because it was
> founded on a rock. And everyone who hears these sayings of
> mine, and doesn't obey them, shall be considered a foolish man
> who has built his house upon the sand. And the rain came down,
> and the floods arrived, and the winds blew and beat upon that
> house, and it fell: and the fall of it was great.

It was a deft move in this parable to end with a metaphor
of two houses, one built on sand and therefore unstable, and
one built on solid rock. It's not a difficult parable, as anyone
can comprehend the metaphor. Sigmund Freud once said that
whenever people dream of a house, they dream of their own
soul. Jesus intuited this, and his two houses are human souls,
one of which has a foundation provided by Jesus — a rocklike
sense of the human condition enhanced by his teaching. Souls

in communication with God should fear no storm, no dislodgment. The wind and the rain will fail to topple (although they might shake) such people. But those with souls built on sand will find it difficult to weather out a storm.

The Parables

Wherever he went, Jesus spoke in parables, and these — in the Synoptic Gospels especially — form the marrow of his teaching. In using parables, Jesus harks back to Hebrew scripture, which provides an array of Jewish parables (Hebrew: *mashal*). In Ezekiel one finds short, pithy statements or aphorisms — a genre that Jesus loved — as well as longer allegorical stories with a twist or moral at the end, the main form of parable that Jesus adapted for his purposes. That they often seem to possess a secret at their core may puzzle some, but the origins of the parable lie in the prophetic books of the Hebrew Bible, and it wasn't foolish to disguise messages in ways that made them less accessible to the larger world, especially during times of exile or political turmoil.

Ezekiel, for instance, was written during the Babylonian exile, when Jews found themselves in a foreign land, at a loss to understand their state. Solomon's Temple had been thoroughly destroyed, and narratives that prophesied the triumph of Israel seemed hopelessly at odds with developments on the ground.[27] The nation of Israel had been uprooted: physically and spiritually. The plot of their story had been rudely disrupted. So the author of Ezekiel and other writings sought a hidden narrative, a buried design that might be grasped in the form of parable. In *The Parables in the Gospels* (1985), John Drury says: "The element of secret knowledge which had always been part of the structure of prophecy came to dominate it. The prophet became a wise man, a dreamer and visionary, an interpreter of dreams like Joseph in his affliction and exile. As such he held the clue."[28]

The parables in the gospels function in a similar way, offering oblique teachings, almost preternaturally evasive in certain instances. In Mark 4:13, for example, Jesus says (perhaps with a slight grin): "You don't know this parable? So how will you know all the parables?" The parable here concerns the sower who sowed his seeds in stony ground. The birds came and ate the seeds; other seeds fell on "good ground," and they yielded fruit in abundance. In the middle of the telling Jesus says: "To you has been given the secret of the kingdom of God, but for those outside everything is in parables." There is a lot of mystification, as Jesus goes on to say that the parables make sense only to those who hear them with the ears of faith; those on the outside can't understand what they hear. Mark observes that Jesus spoke in parables to the people at large, "and when they were alone, he expounded all things to his disciples" (Mark 4:34). Jesus didn't want the people at large to understand his words too easily, "lest at any time they should be converted, and their sins should be forgiven them."

Readers may object: Doesn't Jesus actually *want* his followers to be forgiven? This verse—like so many verses in scriptural writing—needs context for understanding. Mark actually quotes a passage from Isaiah (6:9–10), where God tells his prophet to say to the people: "And he said, Go, and tell this people, Hear ye indeed, but understand not; and see ye indeed, but perceive not. Make the heart of this people fat, and make their ears heavy, and shut their eyes; lest they see with their eyes, and hear with their ears, and understand with their heart, and convert, and be healed." Keeping this passage from Isaiah in mind, one begins to see this puzzling remark of Jesus as yet another attempt by the evangelist to place him, perhaps clumsily in this instance, in the tradition of Jewish prophecy. Mark assumes incomprehension, that the audience at hand will hear Jesus but not understand his words. They will not accidentally "turn and be healed," as their turning would be an intentional act. One must, however, assent *in order to* understand.

The continuously pressured, anxiety-filled historical context of Jews under Roman rule freights the parables of Jesus.
They generate multiple layers of meaning as Jesus attempted to
communicate with people who might resist what he had to tell
them, as with the infamous saying that it's easier for a camel to
pass through the eye of a needle than for a rich man to enter
heaven.[29] Here, as elsewhere, Jesus wished to annoy, even out-
rage, the elite classes, especially those who understood only too
well that this upstart crow sought to overturn aspects of Jewish law, despite his protest to the contrary in the Sermon on the
Mount. His new covenant posed a threat to the old one, making
those who listened nervous. If they dropped everything and followed Jesus, anything might happen.

Jesus spoke fearlessly, unafraid to challenge or upset those
who listened. One senses that edge in his parables, a cunning
that threatens to undermine established opinion and overturn
expectations. He shocked his listeners into fresh understand-
ings, as in the parable of the mustard seed, which appears in all
three Synoptic Gospels. In Mark 4:30–32, it runs as follows:

> What's a suitable image for God's kingdom? What parable might
> I use to explain it? Think of a mustard seed. When scattered on
> the ground, it's the smallest of all the seeds; but when it's planted,
> it grows and becomes the largest of plants. It puts out such exten-
> sive branches that the birds in the sky can nest in its shade.

In other words, something quite massive can grow from
something as tiny as a mustard seed. (The revolt of one person can lead to large political movements, for example. A single
spiritual awakening can precipitate a wave of religious feeling.)
The plant in this parable would be the black mustard, which
grows to nine feet in height. Jews rarely planted these in their
gardens, regarding them as weeds; but one found them abun-
dantly in the fields. The idea of a tree filled with birds suggests

that the kingdom of God would in due course welcome all comers, and that it would grow to a considerable size. Although it grew wild, it flourished under circumstances of cultivation. And it had many health-giving properties. This parable works on a political level: one can imagine Christians establishing a righteous kingdom on earth; it also works on a spiritual level, as the consciousness of the individual Christian deepens into a faith-based community, and one begins to comprehend that Jesus is the vine and we are its branches.

Drury writes of this parable: "Here is an image of the eschatological state or kingdom, a tree full of birds. Eschatology, of a decidedly futuristic sort, as we would expect in the context, triumphs and has the last parabolic word before the editorial conclusion."[30] That "editorial conclusion" follows in the next verse: "With many such parables he spoke the word to them, as they were able to hear it." Drury and many other scholars go to considerable efforts to locate each parable within the developing context of the specific gospel (as well as within the unfolding life of Jesus) and its specific historical setting.[31]

The parables deal with ordinary things, such as baking bread (the Parable of the Leaven) or knocking on a neighbor's door (the Parable of the Friend at Night) or with a mugging by the roadside (the Good Samaritan). In each case, Jesus wished to teach a lesson, make a point about the kingdom of God, or nudge his followers in a more enlightened direction. But it was easier to communicate with familiar imagery—often drawn from rural or village life. As ever, he met people where they were, in their own daily lives.

A fair number of the best parables concern loss and redemption, as in Luke, where three parables on this theme occur: the parables of the Lost Sheep (the shepherd goes out of his way to locate a strayed animal), the Lost Coin (a woman goes out of her way to find a missing coin), and the Prodigal Son—one of the longest and most highly crafted of parables, where a father lavishly welcomes home a son who has squandered his inheritance on wild living in a faraway land. The son returns in a wretched state, barely alive. His father's response is overwhelming: he kills a fatted calf to celebrate the homecoming of this "wasteful" or prodigal son. The son's older brother, however, is not overjoyed by anything that unfolds before him. He has worked diligently beside his father for years. Now he finds the spectacle of his younger brother being feted in such a manner wholly extravagant and surely unearned. Fury and jealousy overwhelm him. But his father speaks to him with calm affection: "Son, you are always with me, and all that I have is yours. But it was fitting to celebrate, for this, your brother, was dead, but he's alive again; he was lost, and now is found" (Luke 15:31–32).

Like others, such as Henri J. M. Nouwen (who wrote a memorable book on this parable), I've stood in awe before Rembrandt's *The Return of the Prodigal Son* in St. Petersburg, Russia, at the Hermitage. One of his last great paintings — he died in 1669 and completed this masterpiece in the two years before his death — it captures the moment of forgiveness and mercy essential to the parable. The bearded father's expression is one of huge relief as he embraces a beloved son who was thought lost but has returned on his knees. His eyes glimmer with love as well as thanksgiving. The resentful older son peeks around a corner, in a darkness that is spiritual as well as physical. His resentment glowers. And yet one feels sorry for him, too. There is a kind of openness to pain in his expression. The light-drenched figures — father and prodigal son — blaze in the foreground. But one grieves for the elder son, who might well be the most important figure in this parable. He, too, is lost and needs forgiveness as well as compassion. The painting reaches forward in time, extending through it, dissolving it. The stillness of the image is indelible, an act of loving attention to a single frame of the parable, the action frozen but kinetic, reflective as well as expectant.

Miracles and Ministry

The personality of Jesus, and his radical incendiary ministry, caught the attention of all who heard about it; his reputation spread rapidly through Galilee, where he dispensed his signs and wonders and spread the "good news" of a coming kingdom with astounding energy. In one of the memorable images of the public ministry, we find him standing in a boat in the Sea of Galilee and preaching to those on shore. Not a fisherman himself, he seemed to enjoy being in boats and often employed metaphors derived from fishing. We even find him walking on water in a moment emblazoned in the memory of most Christians throughout the centuries.

In that scene, Jesus walked toward his disciples during a storm, and yet they didn't recognize him. "It's a ghost," one of them cried (Matthew 14:26). Jesus responded with his typical reassurance and calm: "Be of good cheer; it's me, so don't be afraid." Peter questioned him now, uncertain about the identity of this mysterious figure. But Jesus told him to come toward him. Peter took the risk, walking toward him over the water in a strong wind. When he grew frightened, his faith withering, he sank into the waves. Jesus reached out to him, lifting him up. "O you people of little faith, why did you doubt me?" As soon as Peter resumed his trust in God, he was buoyed up.

The miracle of the loaves and fishes takes center stage in the gospels, for good reason. It's the one where Jesus managed to feed five thousand men and women with just five loaves and two fishes, and there was still leftover food. (In a similar miracle, reported only in Mark and Matthew, Jesus fed four thousand.) It's a miracle of abundance that occurs in the wake of the beheading of John the Baptist, terrible news that would certainly have upset Jesus and spread fear among his disciples. He withdrew to a small boat, grieving the loss of his cousin, who had inspired and baptized him. After a time of intense prayer, God directed him back into the world, where a crowd gathered around him in the countryside. He went straight to work, healing the sick, offering words of encouragement, and preaching the good news of God's love. It grew late, however, and the disciples began to worry about the fact that nobody had eaten. They suggested that Jesus send the crowd into nearby towns for food. Jesus, however, insisted they should stay. Having been handed five loaves of bread and two fishes, he told the huge crowd to sit on the grass. Then he looked up to heaven and, like a magician-priest, broke the loaves and fishes into countless pieces, feeding everyone. Twelve full baskets of food were left over.

The point is that God will meet the needs of his people, even exceed them. It's a message of abundance: there is always enough, even more than enough. Once again, an act of Jesus recalls a famous scene from Hebrew scripture; in Exodus, God (in the presence of Moses) fed the hungry Israelites with manna from heaven, a snow of bread in ridiculous profusion. The Moses link would have been a strong association in the minds of those fed by Jesus as well as those who later listened to this story as it arose in all four gospels, which suggests that it had a key place in the worship of early Christian communities. Whatever they required, God would provide.

Miracles of healing spin through the gospels, a key part of the work of Jesus, and one cannot ignore them.[32] But Jesus emphasized that he himself didn't perform these miracles of healing but that *the faith of the person being healed* mattered a great deal. Jesus was merely an instrument of God, as in the healing of ten lepers in Luke, where he doesn't say, "I did this for you." He says, instead: "Arise, go your way: your faith has made you whole" (Luke 17:19). This is not, I think, contradicted by the passage in John where Jesus told skeptics to believe the works that he accomplished, even if they didn't actually believe he was the Son of God: "Although you don't believe in me, believe the works I do, so that you may know, and really understand, that the Father is in me, just as I'm in him" (John 10:38). Jesus felt the power of God within himself, and he could engender faith in those around him, and this faith had the power to heal.

The End of the Journey

As noted, we can't know exactly how long Jesus and his disciples lingered in Galilee and its environs. But the time came when Jesus himself began to feel the pressure of his destiny, when he saw with absolute clarity that the contours of his life had begun to assume a mythic shape. This understanding may have come to him suddenly or gradually (I prefer the latter), as he walked and preached, healed and comforted. However it came about, he saw that he himself must become a kind of sacrificial, or paschal, lamb. This would be, indeed, the concluding phase of his mission. Jerusalem — the Holy City — now swung into view: he must go there with his disciples, on foot, passing through Judea and Perea. He had something in mind, perhaps inchoate at first but resolving and urgent: an image of himself as Messiah, the anointed one — or Christ. The spirit had been working in him for some time now, enlarging his consciousness, forcing revelations that he would share with those closest to him. He had developed a primal intimacy with God, and the spirit had begun to work, in him and through him, in ways that would affect everyone who came after. "Christ is born," wrote Emerson, "and millions of minds so grow and cleave to his genius."[33] But Emerson understood that the word "genius" only means "spirit" in Greek, and that it flows from Jesus into each us, as when we find in ourselves the divine spark. "Whenever the mind is simple,"

Emerson continued, "and receives a divine wisdom, old things pass away." And so a new world rises with the sun/son, breaking over the horizon, beckoning as we walk in the footsteps of Jesus, stopping by the wayside to listen to his simple, comforting, at times alarming words.

5

Entering Jerusalem

If I forget thee, O Jerusalem!

— PSALM 137

For I also had my hour;
One far fierce hour and sweet:
There was a shout about my ears
And palms before my feet.

— G. K. CHESTERTON, "The Donkey"

IN THE COURSE OF WALKING through Galilee, Jesus acquired an awareness of his sacrificial role: its contours would have slowly become obvious, however disconcerting. In showing men and women how to die, he would show them how to suffer and overcome suffering, with God's help. By the Resurrection he showed a way to conquer death itself. And yet the contours of the *mythos* rivet our attention, especially the anxiety of Jesus in the days before his execution on the cross. The gospels come intensely into focus during the final parts of the story, which begin with the approach to Jerusalem for the Passover festival.

As this major holiday approached, the ground in Palestine must have thundered as tens of thousands made their way toward the Holy City for the annual festival that celebrated the liberation of the Jews from Egypt in ancient times. Jesus and his disciples joined the throng, traveling from Galilee, about a hundred miles to the north, taking a route that avoided the dangerous parts of Samaria and followed the Jordan River—a slightly longer journey but less dangerous, as it avoided roads known for thieves and outlaws who must have regarded pilgrims as easy prey. The usual plan was to spend a week before the holiday in the capital, making spiritual preparations for the Feast of Unleavened Bread, as commanded in Leviticus 23:5, where the word "Passover" occurs—a reference to God's benevolent "passing over" the houses of Jews as he swept through Egypt intent upon killing the young children of families during the period of ten plagues. The feast itself marks, indeed, the special relationship between God and the Jewish people.

The Jesus story only makes sense within the context of devout Judaism. And Galilee was pervasively Jewish at the beginning of the first century. Archaeological research supports this assertion in ample fashion. Excavations, for instance, have revealed an absence of pig bones, which means that the populace kept to Jewish dietary laws. Diggers have found an abundance of stone masonry instead of pottery, as these vessels could be ritually cleansed. Purification baths and other signs of ritual practice were common during this period.[1] There were only a few substantial synagogues in the smaller towns, but this doesn't suggest a lack of piety. One assumes that devout Jews met in houses or public locations, as synagogue only means "a gathering." A fixation with Jerusalem, however, persisted—and the story of Jesus drives toward that physical embodiment of God's kingdom on earth, the Second Temple.

This massive structure drew faithful Jews from everywhere in Palestine for major celebrations, with the population of the city (usually about thirty thousand) swelling by as many as seventy or eighty thousand during the festive week. The magnificence of the Temple itself may have played a part in this: here was God's home on earth, the exact spot where the Holy of Holies and its veil focused the rays of God like a magnifying glass, drawing heavenly energies to a fine point of fire. That it had arisen from the ashes of the First Temple must have given it added significance, making it a symbol of rebirth.

Jesus had been there before, as we know: the glimpse we get of him at the age of twelve suggests that pilgrimages to Jerusalem had been a regular part of his life. Though possibly trained by rabbis in Galilee — nobody knows the extent of this — he had nonetheless quarreled with Jewish authorities, attracting fierce criticism from the Pharisees, in particular, as we have seen. Some of them had petulantly asked Jesus for a "sign from heaven," as if he must somehow prove his legitimacy in the eyes of God. Quite rightly, he showed contempt for this request. Why did he need to prove his Jewish credentials or his connection to God? Of course he filled his sermons with references to Hebrew scripture, making sure that everyone understood that he was a "new" Moses, a prophet in the vein of Judaic prophecy. He made sure that everyone understood that he was a devout Jew. From an early age, he had shown his attachment to the Hebrew Bible and its words — and demonstrated independence of thought with regard to the meaning of actual passages.

A turning point came toward the end of his public ministry on the outskirts of Caesarea Philippi, when Jesus shifted into a self-reflective mood, asking his disciples a leading question: "So who do people tell you is the Son of Man?" The answers he got seem puzzling: "Some say John the Baptist, others say Elijah, and yet others say Jeremiah or one of the prophets." Only Peter understood what Jesus was asking. He replied fulsomely: "You are the Messiah, the son of the living God" (Mark 8:27– 30; Matthew 16:13–20; Luke 9:18–20). Jesus liked this response, saying: "You are blessed, Peter." He added, famously: "On you, Peter, I will build my church [*ekklesia*]" (Matthew 16:18).[2] From this point on, the ministry seems to have a sense of direction, as Jesus wished to build God's kingdom on earth, one that would have a connection to the heavenly kingdom. He seems to have understood, at last, that he must suffer himself, taking on a sacrificial role in the great drama opening before him.

Jesus explained to his followers that he must go to Jerusalem in order to suffer at the hands of the Jewish authorities. Peter objected: "This will never happen to you." Hearing this childish assertion, Jesus lost his temper with his "rock" Peter, saying "Get behind me, Satan" (Matthew 16:22–23). It's important to remember that Satan here means, as usual, the Adversary. Peter simply refused to countenance a suffering Lord and Savior, and Jesus lost his temper with his resistance. But Jesus went further, explaining to his disciples that they must *all* take up the cross with him. For the first time, Jesus appears fully to appreciate — and allow his disciples to understand — that each of the disciples must also become models of suffering, taking up his cross and following him.

The Transfiguration

A week later, Jesus took Peter, James, and John — his closest disciples — to a high mountain, perhaps Mount Hermon or Mount Tabor (the latter is the place most often associated with this event, but the gospels offer no specifics). There he was stunningly transformed or "transfigured." Matthew and Luke copy Mark almost verbatim in relating this major event, with Matthew — the most gifted writer among the four evangelists — adding a few marvelous touches: "And he was transfigured before them, and his face shone like the sun, and his garments turned white as the light itself." Luke describes the garment as "dazzling." Almost at once both Moses and Elijah appeared at his side, and God's voice thundered from heaven, echoing the voice that issued from the heavens at the baptism of Jesus: "This is my beloved son, in whom I am well pleased. Listen to him" (Matthew 17:5).

If anyone had any doubts about the identity of Jesus now, the gospels erase them here. This is the Son of God, and the mystical transformation of his earthly body into a heavenly one prefigures the Resurrection itself. As Thomas Aquinas observed, the Transfiguration shows the disciples, and every Christian, the light at the end of the tunnel: a glorified body. Aquinas used the metaphor of an archer who must see the target before he draws his bow. Aquinas insisted on a bodily resurrection and — like many of the Church Fathers (especially Origen) — regarded the Transfiguration as a central miracle, a glimpse of the world to come. As Norman O. Brown — a New Age prophet of sorts — wrote in *Love's Body*: "Christ is able to project the life-giving power of his glorified body without spatial limitation."[3]

The disciples, especially Peter, found it difficult to absorb the meaning of this vision. Terror had seized them almost immediately upon the arrival of Elijah and Moses, and they fell to the ground. The voice of God had probably added to their amazement and anxiety. Peter, in particular, seemed quite confused as well as eager to do something about what he had seen. He asked Jesus if he might build three "tabernacles" or huts on the spot, perhaps to mark the place where such an astonishing thing had occurred or perhaps to induce Moses and Elijah to stay with them for a while. In fact, Jesus cautioned them to say nothing about what had happened until he was risen from the dead. It's a mysterious turn in the narrative, and it suggests that Jesus wished to keep this a special moment for his closest disciples. He was creating a pact, giving them a preview of the life to come.

As it would, the Transfiguration appealed to many of the great artists. How could anyone with talent pass up the chance to depict the shimmering body of Christ midair between two of the greatest Old Testament prophets? The best example is perhaps Raphael's last painting, unfinished at his death in 1520. In it, Jesus floats before a white cloud, in passionate discussion with Moses and Elijah, who hover only just below him. The disciples lie on the ground beneath the trio, stricken by the radiance. The bottom half of the painting depicts a chaotic world, where Christ in shadow casts a demon from a possessed boy. The two panels interact in subtle ways, with suffering humanity below and the glory of the Transfiguration above. Raphael suggests that the two worlds depend on each other — what the poet Wallace Stevens called "the old dependency of day and night."

On to Jerusalem

Soon after this event, Jesus and his disciples joined the river of people flowing into Jerusalem, pausing to sleep outside of the capital at Bethany — a village to the east of the capital, on the southeastern slope of the Mount of Olives. It was a place known for its poorhouses and leper colonies, a place of disaffection. (In Mark, for example, we hear of Simon the Leper living in the vicinity.[4]) But the landscape approaching Bethany would have had its beauties as well: terraced hillsides, orchards full of almonds and pomegranates and dates, serried trellises where the vineyards produced a sweet, strong drink of garnet-red wine. It was en route to Bethany that Jesus heard from a messenger that his dear friend and follower Lazarus had died.

Lazarus was the brother of Mary and Martha, two women close to Jesus. And this death mattered to Jesus. (The phrase "Jesus wept" occurs in the context of this death, revealing the intense emotion that surrounded the event for Jesus. Nowhere else in the gospels does he weep.) Only John's gospel tells this story, but it's an unforgettable one, narrated at length in the eleventh chapter.

This good friend of Jesus had been ill for some time, and he died. He was immediately buried in a cave, with a large stone rolled over the entrance. Everyone wondered why Jesus, who was such a gifted healer and supposed friend, had delayed his arrival in Bethany. He might have rushed to Bethany in order to save Lazarus, as Martha impertinently reminded him. What was he thinking? Where had he been? Her hysteria didn't seem to move him.

Instead of being drawn into her questioning, Jesus explained to her that he himself was the source of life. "I am the resurrection and the life," he told her. "Anyone who believes in me shall live, even if he dies" (John 11:25). This response to Martha must have puzzled his followers. It suggested to them that something was up, that a transformation or series of transformations lay at hand. Certainly Peter, James, and John, who had recently witnessed the Transfiguration, understood that the time for the fulfillment of biblical prophecy lay near. This would be no ordinary week in the life of Jesus. He now addressed them with a peculiar intensity, in ways that none of them had quite heard before. But what about poor Lazarus?

Jesus led them to the burial cave. But what did he have in mind? Lazarus had been dead for four days. That's a long time to be dead, and the body had begun to stink, as Martha pointed out when Jesus commanded them to roll away the stone. Meanwhile, word on the street had leaked out, and locals rushed to the burial grounds to see him for themselves. He was apparently capable of astounding feats, a first-class healer. But how could he help a dead man? Jesus had, in fact, already raised two people from the dead, the widow's son at Nain and the daughter of Jairus; but the little girl was said to be "sleeping," and the widow's son had only just died. But Lazarus had been really and truly *dead*, and nobody could argue he was simply "unwell."[5]

Jaws dropped as "the man who was dead walked out, with his hands and feet wrapped in bandages." The crowd gaped as Jesus told them to untie the man, to free him, that he was no longer dead. Startled (even panicked) by this deed, observers rushed to tell the Pharisees and assorted Jewish elders what Jesus had accomplished, and they met to discuss this man who performed "many miracles." It wasn't right, they decided. "If we let him carry on like this," they said, "the Romans will come and steal our country and take away our nationality." Jesus had upset the temporal authorities, and political consequences would surely follow. As it were, Jesus had unleashed more than simply a dead man. He had unleashed the vengeance of the authorities; they must somehow control this man who not only challenged their position of dominance but could with his very black magic reverse the effects of death itself. "From that day on they plotted to kill him," we are ominously told.

A prominent scholar called Morton Smith actually regarded the story of Lazarus as an example of ritual acting out of a peculiar kind.[6] In a sort of miracle play, Lazarus — a man who was not really dead — pretended to be dead and got into the burial cave. Then he walked out of the cave to dramatize a spiritual resurrection, Smith suggests. But this strikes me as unlikely, as the Lazarus story makes sense within its full mythic context, as a sign that Jesus had extraordinary power over life and death. Such power would soon, of course, grow meaningful in the context of his crucifixion. John knew exactly what he was doing as he relayed this tale, as Lazarus stands in for everyone who follows Jesus and finds himself raised to new life, admitted to an enlarged mind, enlightened. The image of Lazarus stepping forth from the tomb like a mummy drew on deep mythic archetypes.[7]

As John P. Meier notes, "The raising of Lazarus is the last and the greatest of the 'signs' performed" by Jesus in the Gospel of John, and where it's placed, it might be regarded as the culmination of the public ministry. Meier continues: "In a literary sense, the raising of Lazarus unleashes what follows by pushing the plot forward to its inexorable conclusion" as it moves the story forward from the public ministry to the death and resurrection of Jesus.[8] Indeed, in John, it would seem that the raising of Lazarus is what sets the evil gossip about Jesus afoot, making the Jewish elders nervous about this charismatic young man who seemed to draw so much attention from the crowds. Whatever would he do next?

Immediately after this miraculous feat, Jesus went to the house of Lazarus for a meal, and John emphasizes that Lazarus attended this meal and *ate solid food*: he was not a ghost but a living and breathing body, capable of digesting a meal. Mary (the sister of Lazarus) in a symbolic move broke out a jar of ointment, "pure" and "precious," and she anointed Jesus with it—a gesture of thanks, perhaps, for raising her brother from the dead. She also wiped his feet with her hair in what seems a peculiarly sensuous gesture that defies explanation. The house quite naturally filled with fragrances—food, the ointment, perhaps flowers. This was, indeed, the calm before the storm.

Judas sat at the table that night in the home of Lazarus, and he made a typical ass of himself, complaining that Mary wasted her money on this ointment when it could have been given to the poor. It's in this context that Jesus remarked, in a widely quoted saying, "The poor will always be with us" (Mark 14:7). This wasn't a callous saying but a way of showing awareness that, as in Bethany where they dined that night, one saw a great deal of poverty. The fallen world would persist until the end of time, or until rescued by God. Poverty (material and spiritual) would taint the world until the kingdom arrived in the fullness of God's time. This remark by Jesus was also a swipe at Judas, who was a thief and might well steal money destined for the poor.

The Holy City at Passover

The procession to Jerusalem—the name means either City of Peace or Holy City of Peace, depending on your chosen etymology[9]—began with Jesus sending for a donkey (or two, as one of the gospels asserts), saying that he wished for an "ass" and a "colt" in order to fulfill a remote prophecy from the Hebrew

Bible. Leaving Bethany, he felt hungry. Noticing a fig tree by the roadside, "in full leaf," he wondered if any fruit hung there. There was nothing like a good fig to satisfy hunger. But when he found nothing but leaves, he grew frustrated and cursed the tree: "May nobody eat fruit from you again!" (Mark 11:12–14). By the next day, the tree had "withered from the roots."

This episode seems hard on the poor fig tree. But we must take the cursing in context. As Jesus left Bethany, he faced the prospect of his own death by painful execution and knew it; the air around him shimmered with a sense of anticipation. One of his disciples would soon betray him. The fig tree had symbolic resonance, a living organism that had seemed to blossom but not borne fruit: a version of Judas, although in a wider sense it stands in for all faithless people.[10] And Jesus would soon say: "I am the vine, you are my branches" (John 15:5). He represented a living vine, one that bore fruit; he hoped for the body of Christ, meaning his followers, the whole church, to represent a generative system, with live roots and branches, with plentiful fruit. By nature, he was a pruner, and we hear from him that he "removes every branch that doesn't bear fruit, while every branch that does he prunes, so that it will bear even more fruit" (John 15:2). So this cursing the fig tree doesn't, in context, seem quite as impulsive or eccentric or randomly vindictive as it otherwise might.

The gospels say that Jesus entered Jerusalem on a donkey, approaching the city from the Mount of Olives, joining a throng. Onlookers — nobody knows how many — roared with approval, casting palm branches before him: hence Palm Sunday. They treated him like a king, crying, "Blessed is he who comes in the name of the Lord." Centuries before this, King David had also entered Jerusalem on a donkey — as noted in Zechariah. As ever, Jesus behaved in ways that suggest an easy familiarity with Hebrew scriptures; the parallels shaped his behavior. Nothing he did, even entering the Holy City on a donkey, lacked symbolic thrust or precedent.

Coming into Jerusalem in this fashion, Jesus laid stake to a claim, but not an obvious one. Had he entered on a white stallion, he might have been taken for a warrior-king, a latter-day Judas Maccabeus. Some wished that he would actually take on this explicit political role, wanting him to proclaim a new and definitely *political* kingdom, a Jewish state with himself in charge, perhaps. But the kingdom of God was—although not exclusively—an interior realm. All of this remains a complicated matter, however; Jesus may not have wished to overthrow the empire of Rome, nevertheless he had something in mind that attracted any number of political revolutionaries during his own time and long after, as in Liberation Theology, which swept South America in the mid- to late twentieth century with its passion for justice, its call for an earthly kingdom that mirrored the heavenly one. Christians must keep in mind that while the kingdom was and remains a spiritual reality, it has political and social aspects. Jesus addressed and lifted up the materially poor and well as the spiritually poor. He could imagine a state in which human beings and God ultimately reconciled, and this had a political side to it—which is why the Romans did, indeed, execute him. As John Howard Yoder has said in *The Politics of Jesus*: "The liberation of the Christian from 'the way things are,' which has been brought about by the gospel of Christ, who freely took upon himself the bondages of history in our place, is so thorough and novel as to make evident to the believer that the givenness of our subjection to the enslaving or alienating powers of this world is broken. It is natural to feel Christ's liberation reaching into every kind of bondage, and to want to act in accordance with this radical shift."[11]

Word spread quickly that the extraordinary healer and radical teacher, Jesus of Nazareth, had arrived in Jerusalem for Passover week, but it's possible to overestimate the impact of this entrance. Think of the vast crowds moving along the dusty streets, mostly on foot yet some in carts or other crude vehicles, perhaps a few on horseback or camel. How insignificant one man on a lowly ass must have been, except among a discrete band of followers who layered his path with palms and sang his praises. This was hardly a momentous occasion — not going on outward appearances. Jesus was more a rumor in his own time than a legend.

Had this unusual rabbi and healer blended in with the pilgrims who converged on Jerusalem, the story would have ended there. But he made his way to the Second Temple several times within a few days, calling attention to himself, creating a stir. On one occasion, recorded in all four gospels (and therefore central to the teaching of the early Christians) he strode into one of the outer courtyards where livestock milled about and moneychangers sat at long wooden tables. They probably exchanged Greek and Roman money for half shekels, which could be used to pay the Temple tax by pilgrims. In nearby stalls one could buy turtledoves or pigeons for sacrifice: a lucrative business for a handful of merchants. In short, a bustling commercial scene would have been found at the Second Temple, unremarkable in every way.

Jesus swung his eyes around the courtyard and, unusually for him, lost his temper. He fashioned a whip from cords and, in a bold gesture, lunged at the moneychangers, overturning their tables, upsetting the pigeon stalls. "My house shall be called the house of prayer," he shouted, "but you have turned it into a den of thieves" (Matthew 21:13). Some questions remain: Why did Jesus find the activity of money changing so objectionable? Why did he act violently, when he himself had always preached against violence? Doesn't such a tantrum make us think less of him?

Consider the situation. The money changers had monopolized the half shekel, a silver coin about the size of a quarter in American money. Because it didn't bear the image of the Roman Emperor, with its typical inscription "Son of God" (which referred to the emperor), it was deemed appropriate for paying the Temple tax. Yet a feeling of injustice upset the pilgrims, as well it should: these sharks gave them a raw deal, profiteering from their poverty. It's worth noting that the *only* time Jesus ever flared into violence was in reaction to monopoly profiteering. This activity violated his sense of God's full sovereignty. Here was a house of prayer, not a place for making money or swindling pilgrims. And the violence, of course, seems largely symbolic — overturning tables. One doesn't read that he drew blood. It's more like civil disobedience than violent revolution, not unlike the salt march of Gandhi and his followers in the spring of 1930, where many of those in the Indian protest movement set fire to British cloth to symbolize resistance or flung fistfuls of salt distilled from the sea by their own hands into the air to say that they could make salt if they chose, despite the British ban on salt production. People want to control their own economic lives, and when this doesn't happen, the ground is ripe for revolution.

As Jesus left the Temple in a state of agitation and excitement, he looked briefly over his shoulder, saying, "See these great buildings? Not one stone will be left on another. Each will be thrown down" (Mark 13:2). To many ears, this sounded like sedition, and both awe and terror rippled through the crowd. (A major debate swirls around whether Jesus actually prophesied the destruction of the Second Temple that would occur in 70 CE or if, after the fact, later writers inserted this pronouncement. Since probably none of the gospels predate 70 CE, the latter seems like a plausible explanation.) Jesus also said, "If you destroy this Temple, in three days I will raise it up" (John 2:19). Yet we're also told that the Temple he talked about was his body, which he regarded as a sacred space. No doubt this comment foreshadows his death and resurrection, which were accomplished in three days.

The Jewish authorities didn't like what they heard about this exorcist and magician from Nazareth, who counted a Zealot (Simon) and possibly a member of the terrorist *sicarii* (Judas) among his followers. Soon the high priests met with the Sanhedrin, the governing body of judges, to discuss the problem at hand. This was no small deal, as this august group (Greek *synedrion*, which means "sitting together") consisted of seventy-one men of considerable distinction. They met each day in the Hall of Hewn Stones, which adjoined the northern wall of the Temple in a symbolically intermediary space, halfway between the inner sanctuary and an outer court, where it pronounced on legal matters (including punishment for crimes), deriving its authority from within the sanctuary itself, with the Holy of Holies not far away.[12]

The authorities sent spies to investigate the situation, and they approached Jesus in the guise of ordinary folk with straightforward questions. "You're not swayed by what people say. You don't care who they are, but you teach what is true to God." He listened in silence. The spy continued in his apparently guileless fashion: "So is it right to pay the imperial tax to Rome? Yes or no?" Jesus saw through these tactics at once. "You're trying to trap me," he said. "Bring me a Roman coin." They handed him a denarius, which would have borne an image of Caesar. With absolute clarity, Jesus said: "Give to Caesar what belongs to Caesar. Give to God what belongs to God." It's no wonder the spies stepped back and "marvelled" at his response. This clever fellow had outfoxed them.

Although he posed no obvious threat to either Roman or Jewish authorities, the political implications of his teaching eluded no one in power. Yet when the Pharisees asked him about this kingdom that he preached, demanding to know its exact location, he responded: "You won't find the kingdom of

God by looking around. You won't say: Here it is, or there it lies" (Luke 17:20–21). The kingdom of God was coming, and would bring with it a political revolution that enfranchised the poor, although its spiritual dimensions probably meant as much or more to Jesus, and he did not wish to focus his message too narrowly. He hoped to enlarge the minds of those who followed him, to convey a message of all-embracing love that rose above time and place. "The kingdom of God is within you," he said, yet this knowledge created a yearning for justice in those around him. It offered a taste of freedom.

Remember that Palestine languished under occupation by Rome, which kept a wary eye on the Jews, allowing them a measure of self-government, but only within discrete bounds. The Jewish-Roman conflict would, within four decades, boil over, leading to the destruction of the Second Temple and the burning of Jerusalem. In the time of Jesus, many Jews hated the Romans, who maintained a large presence in the capital, with centurions on the streets, and with reminders of Roman rule everywhere in symbolic abundance. This empire governed by force and cruelty, never hesitating to use extreme violence to control those within their command, however distantly supervised. No Jew felt terribly free in this society.

The Last Supper

Meanwhile, the disciples of Jesus innocently wondered where they would eat their Passover meal. Without prior arrangements, they could have been forced to dine in the streets with the poorest of the poor, and they wished to avoid that, having walked a good distance to get to Jerusalem in time for this feast. Jewish law required them to take this celebratory meal within the confines of the Holy City, so they could not simply retreat to Bethany, where friends such as Lazarus and Martha would have welcomed them. In a strange move, Jesus told one of his followers to go into the old city and look for a man with a pitcher of water. He was told to say, "The rabbi wishes to know the whereabouts of his guest chamber, where he can eat his Passover meal with his disciples. And he will show you an upper room furnished and ready for the occasion" (Mark 14:14–15). One gets the sense that Jesus, knowing the plot of his own story, had arranged everything in advance.

Jesus and his disciples gathered in an upstairs apartment known as the Upper Room for the Last Supper or the Lord's Supper—both names eventually attached to this memorable dinner, though the gospels don't use either. The thirteen reclined, men only, around the table, which would have been close to the floor, with cushions around them for comfort: this was the traditional way to dine, although the image of the group sitting upright at a long table has been driven into the collective mind by Leonardo da Vinci's *The Last Supper* (1498), one of the most recognizable paintings in the world.[13] It would have been a tense evening, given the events of the past day and the drama that, upon entering Jerusalem, hinted that something momentous lay ahead.

That this meal would form the backbone of liturgical practice in the coming millennia never occurred to the disciples, who had no plan to start a new religion. Certainly nothing prepared them for the events of the coming days, which unfolded with terrifying speed, a blur of events that would play a huge role in the history of the world from this time forward. They assumed a simple Passover meal, or *seder*, would take place that night in the Upper Room, and nothing more, even though Jesus had kept this an all-male event, a divergence from the usual practice.[14] He clearly had something in mind.

Jesus began the meal by taking off his tunic, putting a towel around himself, and washing the feet of everyone present: a humiliating act, as slaves normally performed this task. Peter, as he would, objected to the idea that Jesus would assume this subservient role. He obviously hadn't yet taken on board the idea that the first should be last, that the meek would inherit the earth. In his limited awareness, he failed to register that compassion and service lay at the core of Jesus's teaching, with humility as a defining virtue; "the poor in spirit" would be truly the blessed.

Accounts vary in Mark, Matthew, and Luke as to what exactly Jesus said as he broke the bread and shared the wine during this final meal with his disciples, but he clearly suggested that the bread represented "his body," and he asked that in the future his followers should break bread in memory of him. With the cup, he "gave thanks" and said: "Drink this, all of you, for this is my blood of the new covenant, which is poured out for many for the remission of sins" (Matthew 26:26–28).

The Eucharistic meal is central to Christian practice, as Paul would later explain to the church in Corinth: "As often as you eat this bread and drink from this cup, you proclaim the Lord's death until he comes" (I Corinthians 11:26). Jesus himself approached the notion of his body as the bread tangentially, leading up to this moment by framing the concept at early moments in his ministry. In John, for instance, a kind of Eucharistic discourse follows the feeding of the five thousand, where Jesus declares: "I am the bread of life" (John 6:48). Certainly Jesus valued the act of recollection (Greek: *anamnesis*), substituting the usual remembrance of the Passover with recollections of the Crucifixion and Resurrection. The Last Supper prefigures meals where Christ, after the Resurrection, would appear again, as if to confirm and recapitulate the notion of a communal feast with symbolic importance. The Roman Catholic scholar Raymond E. Brown observes: "A sacral meal eaten only by those who believed in Jesus was a major manifestation of *koinonia* (communion) and eventually helped to make Christians feel distinct from other Jews."[15]

In John's version of the Last Supper, Jesus offered a final sermon to his disciples (John 13–17) in what is often called the

Farewell Discourse, a densely packed lesson in Christology tinged with Greek philosophical themes, a lecture given to "his own" where Jesus seems acutely aware of his coming departure and recalls what he has said and done during his public ministry. He asks his followers to emulate him, even to surpass him. Unlike anything found in the Synoptic Gospels, in John he puts forward an extensive theological lesson in which he explains that he has come to bring "peace" to his followers (16:33) and to create "eternal life," which is a deep experience of God — what the Protestant theologian Paul Tillich, in *The Courage to Be*,[16] called the "God beyond God" that forms our "ground of being" — an idea of God that has, over many decades, struck me as useful, as it shifts away from a physical image of God as "somebody" who is somehow "up" there in heaven, employing a metaphor of depth and amplitude. In truth, God cannot be reduced to any spatial metaphor.

The idea that Jesus existed before the world came into being occurs in the Farewell Discourse, and it's a complex one, suggesting that the Spirit entered Jesus, making him godlike. The philosophical concept itself refers back to the Greek notion of *logos* as a kind of knowledge that informs creation with order. One thinks of the haunting statement in John, "Before Abraham was, I am." Or "I am the way, the truth, and the life" (John 14:6). These two remarks participate in the *ego eimi* tradition: *I am*, in Greek. The term, used by Jesus in seven major statements in John, implies continuous being, being outside of time. One should recall that God said to Moses: "I am that I am" (Exodus 3:14). Eternal life, in this philosophical frame, isn't a continuation of time to another realm. It's a move beyond or around or through time. It's no-time or, better yet, the Eternal Now.[17] As the poet Wallace Stevens writes in "Notes Toward a Supreme Fiction" in what strikes my ear as a wonderful echo of Exodus as well as the Farewell Discourse: "I have not but I am, and as I am, I am."

In the course of his final speech to his disciples, Jesus also mentioned that a comforter would follow after him, a spirit: the Holy Spirit, the third person of the Trinity — a concept that would evolve in the thinking of the church over several centuries, hammered into shape by Tertullian, one of the preeminent Church Fathers. It's not an idea theologized extensively by Jesus, who shied away from dogma. This "consoler" wasn't simply a spirit, which would be the Greek word *pneuma*; instead, it was a Paraclete, a word uniquely used by John, meaning "the One who walks beside" (Greek: *parakletos*). In this sense the Holy Spirit becomes counselor or reassuring companion.

At the concluding point of the Farewell Discourse lies a wonderful injunction: "This is my commandment, that you love one another, even as I have loved you." In putting love at the core of his teaching, Rabbi Jesus put a fresh spin on Judaism, which had been focused on *Do Not Do This or That*. Do love one another, Jesus said. It's much as he stated in John 3:17: "For God sent his Son into the world not to condemn the world, but so that the world might be restored through him." He sent Jesus so that human beings would understand that, through love and reconciliation, atonement or union with God was possible. In fact, Jesus scolded those who wished to condemn others, as when he said (in the Sermon on the Mount) that he who was without sin should cast the first stone. It's important, in fact, to notice that Jesus was not a condemning sort of person. He rarely suggested that others would be damned. The emphasis on hell that has preoccupied fundamentalist preachers from the middle of the nineteenth century onward has very little of Jesus in its overtones.

As the Last Supper ended in the Upper Room, Jesus informed Peter that he would deny him three times before the morning broke and the cock crowed. The others must have chuckled as Peter went into his usual frenzy of disavowal, asserting his loyalty. But this was Peter being Peter, one of the only disciples with a distinct personality. He would always leap to praise the rabbi, eager to show himself the most aggressive defender of the faith, in every circumstance the most avid disciple. Yet Jesus treated him at times with unusual brusqueness, leading him on, drawing him out in uncomfortable ways, although one sees that Jesus loved Peter and enjoyed teasing him.

Judas was another matter. Jesus intimated in what must have been an intensely provocative moment during the meal that one of his disciples would soon betray him. Judas guiltily wondered, "Is it I?" Jesus neither confirmed nor denied this, replying, "You say so." This exchange would have unnerved everyone at the table. A little while later, in a chilling turn that recalls what had happened at the dinner with Lazarus in Bethany only days before, Jesus sent Judas from the Upper Room, telling him he must do whatever he had to do. Judas slipped away, leaving Jesus with only eleven disciples, who probably imagined that Judas had been sent to give alms to the poor, as he seems to have handled the money for the group.

"Get up!" Jesus said abruptly to everyone as the meal ended. "Let us leave here and be on our way." It was as if, suddenly, Jesus felt that his hour had come. The group of eleven dutifully followed him from the Upper Room into the Kidron Valley, walking toward the Mount of Olives, singing a hymn as they proceeded through the torch-lit spring night in Jerusalem. They could hardly imagine, of course, what lay before them: three days of untold consequence for them, for everyone.

6

The Passion: From Gethsemene to Golgotha

After the torchlight red on sweaty faces
After the frosty silence in the gardens
After the agony in stony places
The shouting and the crying
Prison and palace and reverberation
Of thunder of spring over distant mountains
He who was living is now dead
We who were living are now dying

— T. S. ELIOT, *The Waste Land*

I want to be bruised by God.
I want to be strung up in a strong light and singled out.
I wanted to be stretched, like music wrung from a
   dropped seed.
I want to be entered and picked clean.

— CHARLES WRIGHT, "Clear Night"

Agony in the Garden

TORCHLIGHT BLAZED ON the faces of the disciples who followed Jesus toward the Mount of Olives that fateful night before the Crucifixion. They must have wondered where he led them as they sang a hymn, probably the Hallel, taken from Psalms 113–118, a passage that includes praises to God and thanks for deliverance from the horrific years of Jewish captivity in Egypt. "I love the Lord, for he heard my voice, my cries for mercy," they sang. The refrain might have been: "Blessed is he who comes in the name of the Lord." Whatever version of the Hallel they sang, its intent was clear: God once saved his own people from horrendous circumstances, and he would save them again.

All of the disciples understood the threat before them. Their strong rabbi had behaved in erratic ways in public since his arrival in Jerusalem, drawing unwanted attention. Riots had frequently broken out during Passover week, and the Romans had been swift and merciless in their response, as ever. They looked warily on the countless poor Jews who came from the provinces to celebrate — or cause trouble. Crucifixions were commonplace at this time, though any Roman citizen condemned to death could pull rank and get his head severed by a sharp sword, an easier way to go. But Jesus and his followers were Jews, outsiders in their own land, thus liable to the cruelest form of punishment. Perhaps as a consequence of their fragile position, the Jewish authorities didn't take lightly to misbehavior among their own kind. They wished to curry favor with the Romans, and they would turn on one of their own without hesitation: just to confirm their loyalty to the emperor. It was their way of saying, *You needn't fear us.*

As it were, the Garden of Gethsemane (meaning "oil press") was the goal of this parade through a cold, spring night in Jerusalem, although his disciples probably wondered what Jesus had in mind. Gethsemane was, and remains, an unremarkable grove at the foot of the Mount of Olives. Darkness had fallen by the time they got there, and Jesus asked most of them to remain behind as he took Peter, James, and John — probably his closest disciples, as they had been the ones who witnessed the Transfiguration — to a separate corner. He told them to keep watch as he prayed, and soon fell into focused prayer — almost a trance — as he knelt in the shadows. He begged God to spare him from his coming agony and death. Why must he go through with this? Here we see him as scarcely divine at all, not someone who completely and unequivocally understood that if he died he would rise again in three days. Human frailty radiated from him, and the disciples must have shuddered to see him in such despair, exhibiting self-doubt. Had they made a mistake in trusting him?

Sweat rose on the brow of Jesus "like drops of blood," so we are told in Luke. He spoke to God as *Abba*, the Aramaic word for father, an intimate form of address. After an hour of determined, even furious prayer, he gave himself over to God's will, assisted by an angel, who appeared from nowhere to strengthen him. This is, in some ways, the center of the Passion, the moment when Jesus understood that he must die and decided against fighting any longer, acceding to his fate. Perhaps he also realized that he must show everyone else how to die, taking on the role of sacrificial lamb. His grisly execution would make it difficult for anyone ever again to doubt his humanity, however much they might question his divinity.

The three disciples fall asleep while Jesus prayed, perhaps a response to the four cups of wine they would have imbibed as required by Jewish law at the Passover meal. Suddenly Jesus stood over them, scolding Peter for falling asleep: "Wake up and pray that you won't fall into temptation." The implication was that Peter would soon tumble into a spiritual crevice. Jesus said, "The Son of Man will soon be betrayed. Get up!"

Within moments, footsteps sounded on the gravel path, with voices shouting, torches flared. Judas Iscariot arrived with a cadre from the Temple Guard, as well as priests, even a number of Pharisees, who clearly had it in for this upstart who had challenged their authority. Judas walked up to Jesus brazenly and kissed him on the cheek, a signal that had been preordained: the infamous Judas kiss. Jesus said with only the slightest tinge of irony: "Judas, would you betray the Son of Man with a kiss?"

(Luke 22:48). The guards obviously didn't know which man was Jesus, and they only wanted *him* — which points to their interest in his unorthodox religious views and his disruptive behavior in the courtyard of the Second Temple.

In the apocryphal *Acts of John*, the disciple-narrator says: "After the Lord had danced with us, my beloved, he went out to suffer. And we were like men amazed or fast asleep, and we fled this way and that."[1] Not Peter, however. While the rest of the disciples slipped into the shadows and disappeared, he alone challenged the guards, taking out his sword and slicing off the ear of one Malchus, the servant of a high priest. Blood spurted, and the poor man knelt in the gravel path in excruciating pain. Jesus scolded Peter, telling him to put away his weapon: "Those who live by the sword will die by the sword" (Matthew 26:52). Had Peter somehow not understood that violence was never the appropriate response in situations like this? Had he missed the lesson of the Master so completely? In a final act of healing, Jesus touched the wound and restored the ear of Malchus. A number of the soldiers fell to the ground, in awe.

Jesus gave himself up easily, having made the decision to accept his role. He would face his accusers with astonishing calm, going to his death without resistance. "Let the scriptures be fulfilled," he said (Mark 14:49).[2]

The Trials

Having arrested Jesus, they led him to the house of Annas, the father-in-law of Caiaphas, the high priest (John 18:13). It's difficult to know why they went there first. Annas ran the money changing business in the Temple, so he might have relished a confrontation with this man, even though it was against Jewish laws to put a person on trial at this hour. Jesus, of course, understood the illegitimate nature of this interrogation — it doesn't rise to the level of a trial; he responded carefully to all questions, making sure not to say too much. He would save his words for the appropriate occasion.

At some distance, Peter followed, refusing to abandon his teacher. He sat in the courtyard of the house while they questioned Jesus inside, warming himself by a wood fire, utterly dejected. A servant girl came up to him, with a guard. "This is one of them," she said. "He was with him." She spoke with conviction, but Peter objected to her identification: "Woman, I don't know him" (Luke 22:57). She wouldn't give up, however, and returned later, pointing at him. But Peter denied any association with Jesus for a second time. About an hour later, others came into the same courtyard, including a servant related to Malchus, who singled him out. "He is a Galilean," the man said. Peter's accent had apparently given him away. This time Peter feigned utter disbelief: "I have no idea what you're talking about," he said. As he spoke, the rooster crowed; dawn was breaking. Peter recalled the prediction by Jesus that he would deny his Lord three times before dawn, and he "wept bitterly" (Luke 22:62).

A great literary scholar, Erich Auerbach, has commented on this narrative moment: "A scene like Peter's denial fits into no antique genre. It is too serious for comedy, too contemporary and everyday for tragedy, politically too insignificant for history—and the form which was given it is one of such immediacy that its like does not exist in the literature of antiquity."[3] With its sharp dialogue and compressed dramatic content, this scene leaps from the pages of the gospels. Peter seems thoroughly human here: capable of denying his Lord yet equally capable of regret, even chagrin. He seems to have been placed on a pedestal by Jesus—his "rock" on whom he would build his church; but he was also called Satan shortly thereafter—the Adversary who failed to retain the most basic ideas of his teacher. Peter's denial of Jesus adds texture and meaning to the Passion narrative, as Peter stands in for all of us who find it impossible to hold to our beliefs at every juncture, to do the right thing even when it puts us in jeopardy.

The four gospels (and a vast apocryphal literature) provide kaleidoscopic details about the trial of Jesus, in its various phases, some of them contradictory. Matthew delves into the interrogation of Jesus by Caiaphas, the high priest (and son-in-law of Annas). In this version, Caiaphas ends up "tearing his robes" in dismay at the thought that Jesus had committed blasphemy by claiming that he wished to destroy the Second Temple in three days (and rebuild it in as many). When asked about his divine status by Caiaphas, Jesus replied coolly: "You say so." Then he added, in what is almost a quotation from the Book of Daniel: "In a future time you will see the Son of Man sitting at the right hand of God and coming in the heavenly clouds" (Matthew 26:64). Had Jesus suddenly recalled the prophecy in Daniel about a Son of Man who would fly to heaven and meet the Rock of Ages above the clouds? His indirection stands out markedly, here as elsewhere in the trial scenes.

The responses that Jesus gives to specific questions about his divinity vary in the four gospels, so do the interrogations and trials. In John, the high priest himself — without witnesses or anyone else but a guard present — examines Jesus briefly and turns him over to the Sanhedrin. In that gospel, the guard slapped Jesus for being rude in response to the priest, although no other evangelist mentions this rather shocking moment. As ever, it's worth remembering that we have no coherent narrative thread to follow but various windows, some of them cloudy, through which we look at the life of Jesus.

The arrest and interrogation took place after dark, making anything that happened illegal — religious and civil laws forbade nighttime trials, as noted above. By morning, however, Jesus stood before a gathering of elders and priests, who sat in severe judgment. This was not a civil but a *religious* court, for Jews only. In Luke 22:66–71, we read what happened:

> And as soon as day came, the elders and the chief priests and scribes sat together, and Jesus was led into their council. They said: "Are you the Messiah?" He said: "If I reply, you won't believe me in any case. And you won't let me go, even if I ask. In the future, the Son of Man will sit on the right hand of God." They said to him: "So are you the Son of God?" He replied, "You say so." They responded: "Do we need any more testimonies? We've heard this from his own mouth." So they led him away to Pontius Pilate for official trial and condemnation.

Pontius Pilate — a minor official whose name echoes in the corridors of history because of his part in the trial of Jesus — was in fact the fifth Prefect of Rome to rule in the province of Judea, a representative of the emperor. His historicity is not in question, as he is mentioned in several contemporary sources, and recent archaeological finds, such as the Pilate Stone (an inscribed limestone block found at Caesarea Maritima and now on display at the Israel Museum in Jerusalem), have confirmed his existence.

As they would, the Roman authorities looked askance at Jewish rituals and practices, especially with a flood of pilgrims overwhelming the city at Passover. Given this scrutiny, the Jews hoped to keep prying Roman eyes away from their doings. To play it safe, any *political* rebel was handed over quickly, and the legendary Barabbas — a criminal whom the crowd would asked to be freed instead of Jesus — was probably an example of someone in this category.

Before a Jewish court, it mattered that Jesus should be condemned for blasphemy, for claiming to be God's son. His true crime lay there. Once he came before a Roman judge, however, this charge made no sense: What did they care about his religious views? The Jews could sort out this problem among themselves. So the charge shifted: the Jewish council put Jesus forward as a traitor, a civil threat, possibly an insurrectionist with royal pretentions. Now *that* would pique the interest of Roman authorities.

At this point in the Passion narrative (as relayed by Matthew) Judas appeared unexpectedly before the gathering of priests and elders. Mortified by his guilt, he threw the betrayal money at their feet, then "went and hanged himself" (Matthew 27:5). The exact price paid to Judas for his crime had fulfilled a dire biblical prophecy about a "good shepherd" who broke the bond between Judah (namesake of Judas?) and Israel; "thirty pieces of silver" was the exact price of that betrayal (Zechariah 11:12). Did the gospel writer insert the price himself, working the association with Hebrew scripture? It's impossible to know; but the legend of Judas has loomed in the collective memory of the world, endlessly revisited.

One thinks, for example, of a poignant moment in J. D. Salinger's *Catcher in the Rye*, where young Holden Caulfield talks with Arthur Childs, a Quaker schoolboy, and speculates about whether or not Jesus would have sent Judas to Hell by way of punishment for his betrayal: "I'd bet a thousand bucks that Jesus never sent old Judas to Hell." Holden understands that pity and compassion played a huge role in the life of Christ, and it seemed (at least to him) unlikely that such a sweeping condemnation would occur. In the lore of Western literature, Judas stands in for sinners who feel beyond redemption, those condemned by their own foolishness, their greedy assumption that whatever they do is without consequences. Like Holden, we can't believe Jesus would damn Judas, as it means he might damn us.

Accounts of the trials of Jesus face into a textual storm, as the four gospels harmonize badly here. One suspects that, writ-

ten decades after the fact, it was impossible to get the story
straight. The trials took place behind closed doors, and it's
probable that little of what we read has much historical basis.
In any case, the symbolism rings true: Jesus found himself out
of religious bounds, an enemy of his own people, the Jews, who
sought conformity with Mosaic laws. And what *was* Judaism
without these laws? A man who flouted them was dangerously
astray. Even worse, from their viewpoint, he argued that a new
covenant between God and humanity now existed. This posed
a distinct threat to the established order. Furthermore, Jesus had
proved himself a scoundrel, speaking to whores and infidels,
lepers and madmen. He picked corn on the Sabbath and dis-
missed the arguments of Jewish elders with wry asides or blunt
assertions. He called himself the Son of Man as well as the Son
of God. Did they need more evidence than this that Jesus of
Nazareth deserved punishment, even death?

After his interrogation by the high priest and elders, Jesus — by now exhausted, as he hadn't slept for a day — was sent
to Pilate for a civil trial. (The high priest and Roman prefect had
worked together for many years, so this would hardly have been
the first time that they condemned a rabble-rouser to death by
crucifixion.) Matthew tells the story quite simply: "Now Jesus
stood before the governor, who asked him directly: 'Are you the
King of the Jews?' To this, Jesus answered: 'So you say'" (Matthew 27:11). Once again, Jesus turned the question back on the
questioner: a familiar trope that suggests an odd combination
of coyness, cleverness, and humility. Pilate now asked with genuine sympathy: "Have you heard all the bad things they've said
about you?" Standing motionless, Jesus refused to answer. No
wonder the governor "marvelled greatly" that a prisoner could
be so restrained under the circumstances. Did he not realize the
extent of his jeopardy, the hideous consequences that would
follow?

A turbulent crowd gathered outside the palace, and one gets

a sense of tension and high drama as they called for Jesus to die, perhaps prompted (even bribed) by the Jewish elders themselves. He had upset their Passover celebrations, threatening their very existence. And Pilate was the official entrusted with decisions involving capital punishment, although Herod Antipas — the client king in the region — might have had an advisory role. (Only in Luke does Pilate actually try to enlist the king himself, and not much is made of this. It would have been an unlikely gesture, in any case. Kings had better things to do.)

In Matthew's retelling, the exchanges between Jesus and Pilate leap from the page into our collective memory. The conversation went roughly as follows:

Pilate said: "So — you're the King of the Jews? Is that right?"

Jesus replied: "Is that your idea or did the others tell you about me?"

Pilate answered with a question of his own: "Am I a Jew?" In other words, he wondered: *How would I know what they're complaining about? Do you think I consult with them or comprehend their theological problems?*

When Jesus failed to respond, Pilate took a different tack: "Your own people and the high priests brought you to me. So what have you done?"

"My kingdom isn't of this world," he said. It was a puzzling comment in this context.

Pilate raised an eyebrow: "You're a king, then?"

Jesus answered: "You say so. In fact, I came into this world to tell the truth. Everyone who sides with the truth listens to what I say."

Then Pilate asked: "So what is truth?"

The questions resound to this day, a preoccupation of philosophers, who have devoted a whole branch of inquiry (epistemology) to that matter. Yet no response came from Jesus. Was the question too difficult or did he simply wish to disengage at

this point, being aware that Pilate would not in any case listen
to his response? The silence of Jesus appears to have troubled
Pilate, however; he felt sympathetic toward this man who de-
flected his questions in such a gentle (if puzzling) fashion. He
went back outside and told the crowd that he saw no reason
to condemn this person, adding that it was customary to release one man during Passover. He suggested that perhaps Jesus
might be that man.

They shouted: "Give us Barabbas!"

Jesus Barabbas awaited execution for inciting political insur-
rection (according to Mark, he had killed a man during a revolutionary skirmish).[4] An oddity sticks out: Barabbas shared
the same name with Jesus of Nazareth, as *Bar-abbas* — by its
etymology, absorbing the Aramaic word *abba* — simply means
"son of the father." In effect, Pilate said to the crowd: I'll give
you Jesus the Son of God or Jesus the Son of the Father. It's difficult to know what to make of an obvious wordplay like this.
Perhaps the gospel writers wished to make a point: Jesus the political revolutionary could walk free, not Jesus the blasphemer,
the Son of Man. This irony might have played well in the first
century, especially during the period of the Jewish-Roman wars
that led to the destruction of the Second Temple. It seems lost
on our ears now.

Pilate had no choice but to act, as he understood that pla-
cating a boisterous crowd was half the job of governance. But he
temporized, and had Jesus flogged or "scourged," as they called
it: a particularly gruesome punishment in which they strapped
a condemned man to a post, upright and naked; they thrashed
him with a whip called a *flagellum*, which had small iron balls
and pieces of sheep bones attached to make it all the more de-
structive. This scourging would have left Jesus in a state of horrendous shock, his skin in ribbons, probably unable to walk to
the place of execution, let alone carry a heavy cross. From what

we read, the Roman guards tortured Jesus with relish, digging a crown of thorns into his scalp after the flogging ended. They dressed him in a purple robe to mock his claim to kingship.

Pilate hoped this would satisfy the mob as he brought the tortured man onto the esplanade — a pavement outside the palace. (Jews would not step inside an official Roman building during Passover week in any case, as it would have defiled them. And no doubt Pilate would never have allowed them in.) "Here is your man," he told them. Perhaps they would walk away now, satisfied?

This wasn't to be, as everyone shouted: "Crucify him! Crucify him!"

Pilate said: "You may take him and crucify him, but I can find no basis for this charge."

They would not listen and called: "He claims to be the Son of God, and we have a law that forbids such a claim." The scriptures clearly stated that anyone who led Israel astray by offering "signs and wonders" or acted as a false prophet should be condemned to death by stoning (Deuteronomy 18:20–21). Only death would satisfy their bloodlust.

The fury of the crowd frustrated Pilate, who took Jesus inside for further questioning, as if unable to pull the trigger. "Where do you come from?" he asked.

Jesus said nothing.

"You refuse to speak to me?" Pilate asked. "Don't you realize I could release you — or crucify you?"

Jesus replied: "You'd have no power over me if God hadn't given you this power. And the people who handed you over to me are guilty of an even greater sin."

Pilate wished to let Jesus go, but the Jewish crowd would not relent. So he gave in, washing his hands before the crowd and saying, "I am innocent of the blood of this good person" (Matthew 27:24). In reality, Pilate was a brutal man who had sent hundreds to their deaths by crucifixion. Many at the time — Philo, for instance — regarded him as a thug who would execute people in whimsical fashion, without the bother of a trial.[5] But Pilate has consistently been portrayed by Christian tradition as a man who put Jesus to death with reluctance — probably an effort on the part of later followers of Jesus not to alienate potential converts who were not Jews.

As a means of execution, crucifixion was especially gruesome, reserved for non-Roman citizens, including slaves and Jews. They beheaded Roman prisoners with a sharp sword, as that seemed merciful. Yet crucifixion had been a common practice for hundreds of years going back to the Seleucids and Carthaginians, who passed this brutal practice along to the Romans. Was there a better way to terrorize those who might wish to rebel than to erect ghastly crosses along the roadsides, where the bodies attached to them would rot in the sun for days or weeks, the carcasses picked apart by birds or wild animals? They strapped or nailed the condemned man to the cross and allowed him to expire slowly — and the longer it took for him to die, the better. (Women were rarely crucified, for a variety of reasons, including modesty: it was not a good thing to reveal a naked woman's body.) Dehydration would eventually kill the condemned man, if nothing else did, but his body would have already suffered horribly from scourging, and internal injuries as well as superficial wounds would (with a bit of luck) have produced death from bleeding. The practice continued until banned in 337 CE by the Christian emperor, Constantine, out of respect for Jesus.[6]

The crucifixion of Jesus confirmed that his offense was technically against Roman, not Jewish, laws. And the spectacle would have attracted attention. According to the gospels, Jesus was crucified at Golgotha, a windswept hill outside of the old city walls, described as "the place of the skull" (Greek: *kraniou topos*).[7] The King James translators anglicized the Latin form of the word (*Calvariae*) to Calvary, hence the usual Christian name for the place of execution. The spot lay close enough to the city so that people coming and going could read the mock inscription put over the cross in Aramaic, Latin, and Greek: "Jesus of Nazareth — King of the Jews" (John 19:19–20).

Jesus either carried the cross himself, as John reports, or had assistance from one Simon of Cyrene — described by Mark as the father of Rufus and Alexander — which suggests that the early Christians knew these people and would have nodded, thinking: Ah, *that* Simon! My guess is that Jesus would scarcely have been able to carry a heavy cross, given the tortures he had already endured. Perhaps he took a few steps before he collapsed, in a daze of confusion, in unimaginable pain, with shredded skin on his back and legs, his scalp bleeding. But he could probably manage no more.

One can't know the exact route or the details of what happened along the way to the site of execution, but a vast liturgical tradition has evolved that Christians refer to as the Stations of the Cross, marking fourteen points in the anguished journey of Jesus from the moment of his condemnation to death and burial. These are focal points for meditation on the Passion — the word used for the suffering of Jesus from the Garden of Gethsemane to his death, a period of bleak hours rich in their complexity and symbolic meaning. The trek to Golgotha itself becomes a focus for Christians on Holy Thursday, in particular, and devout pilgrims to this day will sometimes crawl on their knees along the reputed path of Jesus on this journey along what is called the Via Dolorosa.

One can hardly bear to imagine the horrific scene at Golgotha itself, where Jesus opened himself to his fullest humanity, in suffering and sacrifice, with vultures circling in the sky and a dismal or distracted crowd of soldiers and passersby waiting for the end of the humiliated victim. At least his suffering was relatively brief: the Passover approached, and nobody wanted the execution to drag on, as it might incite discord, even revolt, among the Jewish pilgrims, who already felt disrespected by Rome. Better for it all to end quickly.

They crucified two "thieves" with Jesus that same afternoon, one on either side of him. In fact, they were probably revolutionaries or insurrectionists like Barabbas, precursors of the Zealots or other rebel groups who flowed into capital at this time of year, hoping to incite resistance. Accounts of these two fellow sufferers vary from gospel to gospel, but in Luke (23:39– 43) they become the Penitent Thief and the Impenitent Thief. The latter thief mocked Jesus: "Are you not the Messiah? If so, save yourself and us, too." The other scolded this man for his impertinence: "Have you no fear of God, for you are subject to the same punishment? And we have been condemned for good reason, for the sentence we received is commensurate to our crime, but this man has done nothing wrong." Then he added, beautifully: "Jesus, remember me when you come into your kingdom." Jesus replied: "Truly, I say to you, today you will be with me in paradise."

One is so used to paintings and films of the Crucifixion that it's difficult to keep in mind that the gospels give us very different details of this event, creating a more complex picture when taken as a whole than when read as individual accounts. A few women watched from nearby: Mary, the mother of Jesus, Mary Magdalene, and yet another Mary, the "wife of Clopas," the latter mentioned only in John 19:25. (She might have been an aunt to Jesus, although nobody knows for sure.) In Luke, we hear only that some followers watched from a distance, perhaps afraid to come too close, as they might be taken for coconspirators. The account in Matthew — as usual — is more florid and particularized, with lots of people coming and going: Roman soldiers (casting lots for Jesus's clothing), Jewish leaders, and random onlookers. The Beloved Disciple — that mysterious figure — appears in John, and Jesus tells his mother from the cross that this person will look after her when he is gone. "From that point on, this disciple took her into his home," the evangelist explains (John 19:27). It's a touching detail, suggesting that the attitude of Jesus toward his own family had shifted by now.

Moments before his death, Jesus remarked in agony, "I am thirsty." In a sadistic turn, the Roman soldiers put a sponge soaked in vinegar to his lips, bringing on such despair that Jesus could no longer stay alive. "It is finished," he said, and died. He simply "gave up his spirit." In Mark 15:33–34 we read: "And when the sixth hour came, darkness covered the whole land until the ninth hour. And at the ninth hour Jesus cried in a loud voice: *Eloi, Eloi, lama sabachthani?*" The saying in Aramaic means: "My God, my God: Why have you forsaken me?" This gospel also quotes the opening line from Psalm 22 — one of the darkest points in the sequence of Psalms, which track a kind of manic-depressive cycle in the spiritual life of ancient Israel. As Richard Bauckham, a leading scholar of the New Testament, notes: "There is an intertextual network that serves to interpret the Passion of Jesus by setting it within the experience and expectation of Israel."[8] Even in his death, the experience of Jesus — the trajectory of his life — fit a preordained schema. His life and death formed part of a grand mythic cycle.

In saying those words, Jesus also recalled the ending of that psalm, which proclaims: "All the ends of the earth / Will remember and turn to the Lord." The sufferer is vindicated here, restored to his proper place of veneration. As ever, Jesus saw himself as part of the unfolding story of the Jews, and he understood his position as a sacrificial, or paschal, lamb, one whose spilled blood would restore his people, promoting reconciliation with God — atonement.

The crucifixion took six hours, according to Mark. In Luke, the end arrived more quickly, with Jesus saying in a final gasp: "Father, into your hands I commend my spirit" (Luke 23:46). This was on the day before the Sabbath, and "because the Jewish leaders did not want bodies left on crosses during the Sabbath, they asked Pilate to have the legs broken and the bodies taken down" (John 19:31). As it happened, the legs of two "thieves" were broken to hasten their deaths, a technique known as *crurifragium*, but Jesus was already dead, so was spared this further indignity. To make sure he had died, however, one of the soldiers "pierced his side, and out came a mixture of blood and water" (John 19:34). Interpreters have seen this as a symbolic combination of human blood and divine water—one reason that priests, before consecrating the wine, still pour a bit of water into the cup.

A few hours before Jesus died, darkness covered the land, a divinely induced solar eclipse with mythic resonance: the world *should* have gone dark at this time, given the bloody sacrifice of such a person—a symbolism that Jews, whose priests regularly sacrificed animals to signal obedience to the will of God, would have understood in their guts. The theological point of the death of Jesus in such circumstances is framed in Hebrews 10:19–22:

> And so, brothers and sisters, we have the confidence to enter the Most Holy Place by the blood of Jesus—by a new and living way opened for us through the curtain, that is, his body. And since we have a great priest over the house of God, let us draw near to God with a sincere heart and the full assurance that faith brings, having our hearts sprinkled to cleanse us from a guilty conscience and having our bodies washed with pure water.[9]

Jesus died at three in the afternoon, by most reckonings. What followed was a sequence of stunning events, each of them vastly symbolic. The sacred veil that concealed the Holy of Holies in the Temple, for example, was a curtain of about seventy feet in length; it split in two, suggesting that God and humanity would no longer live on either side of a thick membrane. Elsewhere, a number of tombs opened, and a few lucky saints got up and walked around Jerusalem (Matthew 27:50–53). One thinks of those lines in Shakespeare's *Hamlet*, where Horatio notes that after the death of Julius Caesar "the sheeted dead / Did squeak and gibber in the Roman streets." In that same play, an eclipse covered the earth as well, "almost to doomsday."[10] Such arresting details had been circulating for years, and the evangelist must have felt he could draw on this material to amplify his own story.

By Jewish law, a dead person should be buried before sundown, if possible; and it seems that Jesus was fortunate in this case. Two prominent Jews—Nicodemus and Joseph of Arimathea—petitioned Pilate to allow them to remove the body from the cross and deposit the remains in a burial cave that Joseph had already prepared for himself: a hugely generous act on his part. It lay in a quiet garden not far from Golgotha. Although surprised that Jesus had died so quickly, Pilate assented.

Who were these good men, who granted such extraordinary assistance? Nicodemus appears several times in the gospels, always in passing. He was apparently a high-ranking Jewish official. Joseph, too, was probably an elder, perhaps even a member of the Sanhedrin.[11] What remains fascinating is that prominent members of the elite Jewish class should have taken an interest in Jesus, a wandering teacher and healer from Galilee, a man without high connections. He had obviously drawn the attention, and devotion, of a wide range of Jews. This suggests that, far from being estranged from those who practiced Judaism, he was regarded as one of them. We can add to this the information that James, the brother of Jesus, as well as other followers of Jesus, were "continually seen in the Temple" in the days after his death: yet another sign that his position among the Jews was hardly one of severe antagonism, as his followers felt no need to stay away from this holy site.[12] Once again, it makes no sense to divorce Jesus and his movement from a Judaic context; the early Christians saw themselves, mainly, as Jews who wished to modify and extend Judaic practices. They did not intend to create a separate religion.

The gospels describe the Passion of Jesus in shockingly concrete terms, putting his death at the center of the *mythos*. His suffering becomes our suffering, as he models what each of us must face: degradation, loss, humiliation, physical pain, agony, and death itself, the ultimate mystery. Jesus himself explained to Pilate that he believed he came into the world "to bear witness unto the truth" (John 18:37). As one reads the various narratives of the Passion, a single truth becomes apparent: here was somebody prepared to offer an example of how to behave in the face of extreme misery and abuse, torture of the most unimaginable kind. Yet it's more than that, as Abelard, the medieval theologian, suggested, noting that the wisdom of the cross will ultimately be found in a comment by Jesus: "Greater love has no man than that he should lay down his life for his friends" (John 15:13).

This love flowed from God — the origin of all love — but revealed itself in the anguished Christ. So it's only "by the faith which we have concerning Christ that love increases in us, through the conviction that God in Christ has united our nature to himself and that by suffering he has shown us the supreme love of which he speaks," as Abelard put it.[13] Jesus became, in effect, the suffering servant of Isaiah, who was "wounded for our transgressions, bruised for our iniquities," and who by his death would offer life without limit, represented by the iconography of the cross itself, the world tree, which extends horizontally from east to west, which reaches from the pit below to heavens above, an emblem of reality in its vastness, with power converging at the crux, the juncture where the crossbeams of time and eternity meet at what T. S. Eliot called "the still point of the turning world."

7

Resurrection

All faith is resurrection faith.

— HANS URS VON BALTHASAR, *Prayer*

To rise from history to mystery is to experience the
resurrection of the body here now, as an eternal reality;
to experience the *parousia*, the presence in the present,
which is the spirit; to experience the reincarnation of the
incarnation, the second coming; which is his coming in us.

— NORMAN O. BROWN, *Love's Body*

Surely some revelation is at hand;
Surely the Second Coming is at hand.
The Second Coming!

— W. B. YEATS, "The Second Coming"

The Burial Scene

THE BURIAL OF JESUS took place in haste, in keeping with Jewish law, as commanded in Deuteronomy
21:22–23: "And if a man have committed a sin worthy
of death, and he be to be put to death, and thou hang him on a
tree: His body shall not remain all night upon the tree, but thou
shalt in any wise bury him that day." One can only imagine the
eagerness of those who loved Jesus to remove his body from the

cross, a position of extreme exposure and embarrassment, and to lay it gently in a crypt, safe from mocking Roman eyes. At last, the torture was over.

Having acquired permission to take charge of the body, Joseph of Arimathea wrapped it carefully in fine linens and, with the help of Nicodemus, put it in a crypt hewn from rock not far from the site of the execution on the outskirts of Jerusalem. Nicodemus had brought a mixture of embalming spices: aloes and myrrh. One recalls the lines from "We Three Kings," a mid-nineteenth-century Christmas carol:

> *Myrrh is mine, its bitter perfume*
> *Breathes a life of gathering gloom;*
> *Sorrowing, sighing, bleeding, dying,*
> *Sealed in the stone cold tomb.*

A large stone sealed the entrance to the cave: not uncommon in the burial caves of wealthy people in the time of Jesus, as archaeologists have confirmed.

The care taken by these men with the body of their beloved teacher underscored the importance of honoring the dead in appropriate ways. In Genesis, for example, Abraham had been instructed by God to bury the dead only in the choicest of tombs, and so he bought a cave "in the field of Machpelah" in Canaan for the body of his wife, Sarah (Genesis 23:4–19). The law required that even the enemies of Israel, when slain in battle, deserved an appropriate and respectful burial (I Kings 11:15). Moses actually warned his companions that if they didn't follow the laws of God in this regard, they risked being slain and not buried, their corpses left for the birds and wild beasts to pick apart (Deuteronomy 28:25–26). It should not have surprised anyone in the first century that a man whom many considered an important teacher, if not the messianic Son of God, deserved a proper burial.

It was unusual for the bodies of executed men to be buried with respect, however. Soldiers often just tossed the remains into shallow graves or burial ditches, where wild dogs fed on whatever was left. This might have happened to Jesus, as John Dominic Crossan has argued — not, in my view, persuasively.[1] The public would surely have been outraged by such crassness, as Jesus had attracted a sincere (if rather small) following, especially among Galilean pilgrims; with so many visitors in Jerusalem for the Temple celebrations, Pilate would not have wished to unsettle this group, however small by comparison with the others.[2] A discreet burial for Jesus was politically astute as well as in keeping with Jewish customs, and the archaeological as well as written evidence suggests that such burials did occasionally take place after an execution.[3]

Jesus lay in the cave through Friday night, Saturday, and early Sunday: a period of three days, ending with Easter and the Resurrection, known as the Triduum or "three days." Commentators on the life of Jesus often pass over the hours of his entombment, which embrace a painful mental state described in "Waiting" by the Welsh poet R. S. Thomas as "the mind's tree of thorns." But Holy Saturday forms a corridor between the death and resurrection of Jesus, in his remarkable (and theologically complex) passage from Jesus to Christ. Alan E. Lewis, a theologian who wrote a book about Holy Saturday during the final year of his own struggle with terminal cancer, said: "If confidence in the resurrection tends to modify the deadliness of Calvary, likewise it is only those who have first looked into the mouth of hell and seen the world abandoned to its godless fate who then can truly see the meaning of the Easter day reversal."[4] In other words, the *mythos* needs to be heard in two ways — "as a story whose ending is known, and as one whose ending is discovered only as it happens . . . the truth emerges only when both readings are audible, the separate sound in each ear creating, as it were, a stereophonic unity."

Most of us will for a time occupy this anxious, transitional space between two worlds, as described by Lord Byron in *Don Juan* (Canto Fifteen): "Between two worlds life hovers like a star, / 'Twixt night and morn, upon the horizon's verge." Holy Saturday unfolds in this dark space, in the tomb where Jesus lay in a kind of unrealized state, perhaps plunging into psychic or spiritual depths in what has often been called the Harrowing of Hell — a legend without much scriptural basis suggesting that Jesus made a kind of wild descent, with mythic overtones, into the underworld. In fact, mythologies often describe a turn when the hero descends to a deep pit or a place of psychological, spiritual, or physical confinement, as when Jonah spent three days in the belly of the whale or Gilgamesh descended into the underworld in a quest for immortality. Nearly all heroic or mythic tales include a part of the heroic cycle where the hero visits some version of Hell or Hades in his or her quest for immortality (Ishtar, the Babylonian goddess, is a female example). In any case, the Sacred Sabbath, as it's often called with reference to Easter weekend, represents a place where Jesus dives into the darkness before the Resurrection. It lies between two loud claps of thunder, an emptiness wherein we sense a horrifying loss of life, on the one hand, yet remain expectant: in a state of gradually realizing awareness of the life to come. This difficult space is one of the symbolic gifts of the Triduum in its second day: a timeless time that suggests that "God himself has plumbed these depths and has brought creation out of the darkness and into resurrection life," as Richard McLaughlan has written.[5]

Easter Morning and Beyond

Easter morning arrived with a holy hush, the day after the Sabbath, with little fanfare. The gospels pass over the Resurrection, and we never actually see Jesus waken, rub his eyes, stand and stretch. We don't even see the rock that sealed the tomb actually rolled away. The joyous resurrection of Jesus happens off-stage, as it were. The first inkling of change occurred when some of the women close to Jesus came to visit his tomb. The gospel narratives vary on who turned up in the garden first: Mary Magdalene alone or with Mary, the mother of Jesus, and with Salome (Mary's sister or the mother of James and John). In John, the story plays out in suspenseful detail as Mary Magdalene visited the tomb by herself to mourn. To her amazement, she found the stone removed. In panic, she ran to tell Peter and another (unnamed) disciple, who hurried back to the tomb and discovered it empty, much to their distress and confusion. They assumed that someone had stolen the body. Meanwhile, Mary Magdalene sat outside the tomb by herself, crying softly. She could hardly believe the things that had happened in the past few days, and the missing body of Jesus was really too much to bear.

After a while, she returned to the dark, heavily scented crypt, where she "saw two angels in white." They spoke to her, and then a mysterious male figure appeared at her side.

The man said to her in a gentle voice: "Why are you crying?"

She didn't recognize this person and apparently thought he was a gardener.

Jesus responded with a single word: "Mary."

At once she realized who stood beside her: "*Rabboni!*" Her response was in Aramaic, meaning "teacher." The intrusion of an Aramaic exclamation in a Greek text serves to underscore and convey a sense of authenticity. That Jesus would first appear to Mary Magdalene was, of course, a disconcerting matter for some, such as Peter, who must have wondered why he didn't get to meet the risen Christ before her. In three of the Gnostic Gospels — *Gospel of Philip*, *Gospel of Mary*, and *Dialogue of the Savior* — one sees a rivalry developed between Peter and Mary. Elaine Pagels, in her study of the gospels discovered at Nag

Hammadi, notes that these writings outside the canon often "use the figure of Mary Magdalene to suggest that women's activity challenged the leaders of the orthodox community."[6] The raw facts remain: Jesus first appeared to Mary Magdalene. Furthermore, she didn't recognize him.

Nobody recognized Jesus at first — a point of huge significance, as it underscores the difficult and mysterious nature of the Resurrection, which defies all norms and defeats rationalization. The embodied spirit of the Messiah returning from the dead was not exactly the same person who died but some altered version of Jesus, transmogrified more than restored to his former state. In reality, the manifestation of Jesus after his death beggars the imagination: he acquired a spiritual body, as we read in I Corinthians 15:44: "It is sown a natural body; it is raised a spiritual body." There is a subtle teaching here: We should not expect to recognize Jesus at first, even as he wakens within us. (One thinks here of the Buddha, who also awakened to new life in his moment of Enlightenment at the Bodhi Tree, which entails an awareness of Nirvana, a condition of bliss that comes from the blowing out of the three flames of greed, hatred, and delusion.) Recognition takes time, becoming in fact a process of uncovering, what I often refer to in this book as the gradually realizing kingdom: an awareness that grows deeper and more complex, more thrilling, as it evolves.

Jesus walked free of the tomb, appearing to various disciples and followers over the next forty days. One vivid appearance is described in Luke 24:13–32, where the narrator elaborates a story only mentioned briefly in Mark 16:12–13. Two followers of Jesus walked along a sandy road from Jerusalem toward Emmaus. They discussed between themselves the astonishing rumor that Jesus, their beloved teacher, had awakened from the dead. (Obviously word of this occurrence had spread quickly, though nobody quite knew what to believe.) As they talked, a third man appeared beside them, emerging from the shadows.

"What are you talking about?" he asked. They looked at him incredulously: "Are you the only visitor to Jerusalem who doesn't know what's happened?"

They told the mysterious stranger about this "prophet, powerful in word and deed," a man called Jesus of Nazareth, someone who enjoyed a special relationship with God. They retold the story of the women who visited his tomb but did not find him there.

Jesus listened patiently, then scolded them: "You are so foolish, and slow to believe everything the prophets have spoken!"

But even this rebuke didn't alert them to the identity of their companion, whom they nevertheless invited to share their dinner. He agreed to join them that evening. Taking the bread in his hands, he gave thanks for it, "and then their eyes were opened, and they saw who was before them." Somewhat bizarrely, as soon as they recognized their teacher, he disappeared—*poof.* It's a strange but compelling story, suggesting that it's difficult to possess the vision, to retain it. The risen Jesus requires sustained focus, strong belief, and devotion.

Even his closest disciples failed to recognize him, as in the first fourteen verses of John 21, where we hear that he appeared to Peter, Thomas, Nathanael, and two other disciples, one of them the mysterious Beloved Disciple. In the days following the Crucifixion, this cluster of core disciples had returned to Galilee. One assumes they were forlorn, confused, and deeply anxious about their future. Without Jesus to lead them, how would they operate in the world? How would they feed themselves? In situations like this, people often return to familiar habits, and these men were fishermen, so they fished. But the fishing didn't go well.

It was early morning on the Sea of Galilee, and the disciples despaired of catching anything. Suddenly Jesus stood on the shore, although none of them recognized him.

He called in a loud voice: "Friends, not having any luck?"

They explained glumly that no fish seemed to be biting. It seemed quite hopeless.

Jesus offered them a tip: "Throw your net over the right side of the boat, and your luck will change."

They probably wondered: Who is this arrogant man? Haven't we already tried everything we know? Yet he must have spoken with authority, as they took his advice, and their nets filled up at once. They couldn't even drag them into the boat, they so bristled with the catch. It was, of course, a miracle.

Peter suddenly realized — alone among them — who stood on shore. "It's the Lord!" he said with a gasp.

They came ashore warily, however. Who was going to trust Peter? The stranger stood by himself, cooking breakfast over coals. He looked up, offering them bread and fish. His radiance was undeniable. Now they "knew it was the Lord," and yet they scarcely believed their eyes. Was this some kind of trick? Did a ghost hover before them? Had they fallen into a dream-state of some kind?

A larger truth informs these stories. Jesus did not, like Lazarus, simply get up and walk out from the burial crypt and resume life in ordinary time. The Resurrection was not the Resuscitation. As noted above, his closest friends didn't recognize him, not even Mary Magdalene. He was otherworldly now, fully transfigured. What this part of the *mythos* invites is meditation as well as a blunt refusal to accept easy answers, a willingness to submit to the incomprehensible, to what the great German theologian Rudolf Otto called the idea of the holy. Here we discover a sense of the numinous — the so-called *mysterium tremendum* — a "tremendous mystery" difficult to embody in speech or thought, an "all-pervading, penetrating glow" that in its otherness resists the intellect and cannot be discerned easily.[7]

As one moves through the four gospels and the letters of Paul, the accounts of post-Resurrection appearances by Jesus vary markedly in their nature and sequence. There is a summary of these appearances in Paul's first letter to the Corinthians (15:5–8): "He appeared to Cephas [Peter], and then to the Twelve. Then he appeared to over five hundred brothers at one time, most of whom remain alive now, though some have fallen asleep. Then he showed himself to James, then to all the apostles. Finally, he appeared to me."

Written twenty years or so after the events described, this letter suggests two things: a lot of stories circulated about Jesus and the Resurrection, not all of them consistent. These storytellers had their own agendas, and their narratives shifted according to the perceived audience. The author of Mark nearly avoids any mention of post-Resurrection appearances, except for one brief passage (16:9–20), which is not included in the earliest manuscripts of his gospel. In Matthew, there is almost nothing about his reappearance except for a few verses in the twenty-eighth chapter, where Jesus meets the remaining eleven disciples and gives them the Great Commission: "Go and create disciples everywhere, baptizing them in the name of the Father, the Son, and the Holy Spirit, teaching them as I have commanded you. And know that I am always with you, even to the end of time." Luke includes not only the story of the Road to Emmaus but glimpses of the post-Easter Jesus by Peter, plus a further visit with the eleven remaining disciples in Jerusalem. In Acts, which is an extension of Luke, Jesus makes numerous appearances to his disciples during the forty days before he ascends to heaven. In John, he meets Mary Magdalene in the tomb itself, visits with the disciples in Jerusalem, and — as the story related above — meets others by the shores of Galilee, with the miraculous catch of fish: no doubt a symbolic as well as literal catch, perhaps meant to remind these fishermen of their role as "fishers of men" or missionaries who will "catch" men and women with the good news of the gospel. The work of reading here, as suggested earlier, is one of *remythologizing* the story, finding its symbolic contours while not discounting the genuine heft of the literal tale.[8]

The characteristics of the resurrected body of Jesus shift, depending on the text at hand. In one case, Jesus asks Thomas, the doubter, to touch his wound, just to prove to him that he's really there and not some phantasm. This proves that he has a physical presence, and it satisfies Thomas. In John, Jesus passes through locked doors like a ghost — an unsettling image that suggests an incorporeal aspect, stressing his spiritual nature. In Luke 24:41–43, he astonishes his disciples by eating "a piece of broiled fish" as well as swallowing honey. It's as if, by looking at him, they didn't expect as much. He has to prove his real presence. For the most part, the appearances of Jesus retain a dreamlike quality, as in Paul's conversion on the road to Damascus, where he hears a voice from the Lord, which says: "I am Jesus, the one whom you persecute" (Acts 9:5). When Paul opens his eyes, however, he sees nothing. The spirit has vanished.

Huge questions confront anyone thinking about Jesus. Did he *really* rise from the dead? Was there an actual Resurrection? If so, what would that look like? A large number of Christians throughout history have imagined a resuscitation, refusing to countenance the slightest hint that the Resurrection should be regarded as something beyond human understanding. I myself would argue this: life and death are mysterious, at best, and the membrane between the living and the dead is a porous one, perilously thin. Jesus rose from the dead, the scriptures say. I see no reason to doubt this. And yet a literalistic belief in the Resurrection cannot be, as many fundamentalist churches insist, the only important part of the "good news" of Christianity. The message of God's love *in operation in the world* trumps everything and must be regarded as the necessary extension of the idea of rebirth, the social basis for true spiritual enlightenment. Nowhere more so than here does it matter that we find a proper balance between the literal and the figurative, giving full weight to the concrete meaning while relishing the mythic contours of the story.

Jesus put before human beings an example, a way to reconcile with God, the source of creation, the ground of all being. Overall, the Resurrection represents, for me, a joy that is probably diminished by a reading of this event that fails to embrace the mystical aspect, the idea that the transfigured body of Jesus defies human comprehension. Perhaps Doubting Thomas needed a physical manifestation, and some people still do. But the gospel writers repeatedly suggest that the risen Jesus confounded everyone, and that different people regarded this part of the story in different ways — even at the time, among his closest associates. Jesus himself seemed to revel in the mystery, as on the road to Emmaus. He didn't expect, even wish for, instant recognition.

Literalism is reductionist and limits access to God in the fullest sense. I'd go further here to argue that it's downright dangerous to dwell exclusively on the literal aspects of the story. Norman O. Brown wrote in *Love's Body* that the Resurrection should be regard as an awakening, a coming back to life: "The resurrection is to recur, to be fulfilled in us: it is to happen to his mystical body, which is our bodies; in this flesh." This seems, to me, more useful as a way of thinking about the Resurrection than the kind of dour Christianity that argues one is not "saved" unless one "believes" in resuscitation in the most physical way.

The fundamentalist view of the cross, with its emphasis on the sacrificial or "substitutionary" aspect of the Crucifixion, evolved in the Middle Ages and solidified with Martin Luther's insistence on the single, simple, and stable meaning of scripture; the text of the Bible itself became a mighty fortress that resists symbolic interpretations. (I would note that early in his career Luther was much more amenable to symbolic readings of scriptural passages.) To many, the idea of Christ as sacrificial lamb becomes the whole of the Christian message, to the disparagement of every other reading, leading to an exclusionary view of salvation.[9] Yet the apostle Paul himself warned early Christians in his second letter to Corinth that to become an able minister of the new covenant one should not read the scriptures in ways that undercut their fullest meanings, "for the letter kills, but the spirit gives life" (II Corinthians 3:6).

Paul followed his own advice, taking an obviously multi-layered view, as when he suggested that those who follow the way of Christ shall "all be made alive" (I Corinthians 15:22). He wasn't talking about "the dead" here, who required bodily resuscitation. He meant that a spiritual awakening must occur, and this would confer new life on those who understood what they had experienced. It's a feeling not unlike what Thomas Merton, the poet and Trappist monk, experienced in Sri Lanka (then Ceylon) in the late sixties, when he encountered the great Buddha statues in Polunnaruwa: "Looking at these figures I was suddenly, almost forcibly, jerked clean out of the habitual, half-tied vision of things, and an inner clearness, clarity, as if exploding from the rocks themselves, became evident and obvious."[10] This very much echoes the kind of awakening described by Paul.

The Ascension

So forty days after the Resurrection, having made his presence felt, Jesus led his disciples to a hill outside of Jerusalem, at Bethany, where he lifted his hands and blessed them: "And it came to pass that, while he blessed them, he parted from them. He was lifted into heaven" (Luke 24:51). The event occurs only in Mark and Luke, but it's a stunning image, a necessary conclusion to the life of Jesus. Needless to say, the disciples felt utterly at a loss, even bereft. Once again, they had lost their teacher. At this point, an angel spoke to the mystified disciples, saying, "Men of Galilee, why are you gazing up into heaven like this?

This same Jesus, who was taken from you into heaven, will in the same way return" (Acts 1:11). They felt a pervasive joy when they heard these angelic words and returned to the Temple in Jerusalem, where they praised God for this vision of Christ rising to heaven.[11]

The message from the angel refers to the Second Coming, as it's called, which signals the return of the Messiah, embodied in the Greek word *parousia* (which occurs two dozen times in the New Testament, seventeen times referring to an appearance of Jesus). In translation, the word means "arrival" or "real presence." But it also means "manifestation," and can be understood in a variety of ways. Some Christians believe Christ will actually reappear and lift up the dead with him, snatching those still alive from their workaday routines in a dramatic moment called the Rapture. This idea emanates from the Book of Revelation, which has its origins in dream-visions as seen in the Book of Daniel. Daniel, in fact, might easily be considered the first book of the New Testament, with its many influential ideas about the Son of Man.[12]

In truth, the notion of an afterlife that involves bodily resurrection had little currency in the Hebrew Bible. In the Torah, life after death seemed unknown or uninteresting, scarcely worthy of mention. The dead went to Sheol, a shadowy place like Hades in Greek mythology, a kind of garbage dump for souls. Jews, then as now, wished to keep their focus on the present life, leaving what comes after to fate. During the period of the Babylonian exile, however, notions of deliverance for the whole of Israel morphed into a belief in individual resurrection, so that by the second century BCE, when Daniel was written—one of the last books of the Hebrew scriptures—it was thought that the dead might rise in the sky and shine among the righteous "as the stars for ever and ever" (Daniel 12:3).

By the time of Jesus, the Temple elite, the Sadducees, remained firm in their understanding of the afterlife as nothing much; it largely escaped their consciousness, or they preferred not to discuss it. As we read in Acts 23:8: "The Sadducees say there is no resurrection, neither angel nor spirit." It's a view confirmed among Jewish historians, such as Josephus, who wrote, "The doctrine of the Sadducees destroys the souls along with the bodies."[13] The Pharisees, by contrast, developed the concept of bodily resurrection, and this influenced the early Christians, who developed a thoroughgoing notion of survival in some form, with the idea of a "spiritual" or "glorified" body elaborated through the centuries by theologians, especially those influenced by Paul. As for Jesus himself, he explained to his followers somewhat vaguely that when the dead woke up "they would be like the angels in heaven" (Mark 12:25). His teaching focused on the present life, as he argued repeatedly that his true followers must behave in ways that set them apart from everyone else: "By their fruit you will recognize them" (Matthew 7:16). This is amplified and complicated beautifully in James 2:20: "Faith without works is dead." In the Beatitudes, he emphasized that the kingdom of heaven opened *immediately* to those who practiced the virtues he put forward, such as meekness, humility, mercy, peacefulness, and so forth.

Pentecostal Fire

The disciples gathered in Jerusalem ten days after Jesus ascended to heaven, for the Festival of Weeks (Hebrew: *Shavuot*), which was traditionally held fifty days after Passover. Among Greek-speaking Jews, this celebration was called Pentecost, meaning "fifty days," as this marked the passage of time between the liberation of Israel from Egypt and the giving of the Ten Commandments to Moses on Mount Sinai. The Christian feast of Pentecost recapitulates the Judaic tradition here, although it takes on a specific aura of its own.

The disciples crowded in a room in Jerusalem with Mary,

the mother of Jesus, and many other followers. In Acts 2:1–6 one reads what happened, and it's a nugget of narrative enchantment:

> When the day of Pentecost had arrived, they were all together in one place. And suddenly came a sound from heaven like that of a rushing wind, and it filled the house where they sat. And there appeared to them forked tongues like fire, and it hovered upon each of them. And they were all filled with the Holy Ghost, and began to speak with other tongues, as the Spirit allowed. Now Jews and other devout men lived in Jerusalem, out of every nation under heaven. And when this was relayed abroad, the group met together, astounded because every man heard them speak in his own language.

This is the miracle of the tongues, when God sent the Holy Spirit — the third person of the Trinity — for comfort and assistance. A crown of Pentecostal fire hovered above their heads, a flame of hope.

The arrival of the Spirit must have terrified everyone in the room. In "Little Gidding," T. S. Eliot imagines this moment when a "dove descending breaks the air / With flame of incandescent terror." Now, with the spirit of God present in the world, the disciples had a kind of invisible wind at their backs. Needless to say, there is something peculiar about the notion of a ghost who floats into the room as "tongues of fire" and makes its presence felt, allowing a kind of transcendental understanding that cancels out the distinctions of separate languages — the curse of Babel. As ever, one looks for precedents and parallels, which yield a rich literature of speculation about what the idea of the Holy Spirit means.

Raymond E. Brown notes, for example, that the Jewish writer Philo described angels as taking what God had said to

Moses out to the people on the plain below, with the sound of a mighty wind: a mirroring Pentecostal moment in Judaic history.[14] One thinks back to a lovely passage in Numbers, where God assists Moses by giving him and a group of seventy "men of the elders of the people" the assistance of the spirit: "And the Lord came down in a cloud, and spake unto him, and took of the spirit that was upon him, and gave it unto the seventy elders: and it came to pass that, when the spirit rested upon them, they prophesied, and did not cease" (Numbers 11:25). Just as the presence of the Holy Spirit marked a covenant between God and Israel, so the Christian Pentecost signaled a new covenant between God and humanity.

At the feast in the upper room at Pentecost, Peter was moved to deliver a major sermon (Acts 2:14–36), wherein he laid out the essentials of Christian belief, seeing the Pentecost as the fulfillment of signs often given in the Hebrew scriptures, as in Joel 2:28: "And it shall come to pass afterward, that I will pour out my spirit upon all flesh; and your sons and your daughters shall prophesy, your old men shall dream dreams, your young men shall see visions." It's remarkable how the gospel writers, and Paul as well, managed to locate passages in earlier scriptures that reinforced whatever happened in the present. Everything they said or did, much as nearly everything that Jesus said or did in his life, fulfilled a prophecy. Now the Holy Spirit would pour out from heaven, and the men and women in the Jesus movement would dream wild dreams, would entertain lively visions.

The Resurrection engendered a sharp turn for the followers of Jesus. There had, indeed, been other prophets and teachers in earlier years: John the Baptist, for example. But the triumph of Jesus over death shifted the focus from the kingdom of God—often a theme that Jesus put forward in his teaching—to a renewal of life in the moment of "belief." This does not mean—as some Christians will continue to argue—that Jesus wanted people to give intellectual assent to a set of dogmas, thus making it possible for them to be "saved." In its Greek and Latin roots, the word "believe" simply means "giving one's deepest self to" something. The Latin is *credo*: I believe. This derives from *cor do*: "I give my heart." The English word "believe" connects, via root meanings, to the Middle English *bileven*: "to hold dear." And so to believe in Jesus means to hold him dearly, to value his presence and example. As Reinhold Niebuhr, the influential American theologian, once said, belief does not mean that we should claim to know anything about "the furniture of heaven or the temperature of hell, or to be too certain about any details of the kingdom of God in which history is consummated."[15] That would be to reduce the unknowable to something thin and paltry, far too literal to contain the larger truth of eternal life — the good news in its fullest sense.

The early followers of Jesus and, soon, a growing number of apostles and faithful servants, dedicated their lives to bringing the good news to the world, and they succeeded beyond their fondest imaginings in the work of fulfilling the Great Commission. The early church began to organize in different parts of the Roman Empire, with some Christians focused on James, the brother of Jesus, in Jerusalem, while others went as far abroad as Rome and beyond. In the middle of the first century CE, Paul would encounter a vision of Jesus on the road to Damascus, and his brilliant letters to disparate churches in Rome, Corinth, Ephesus, Colossae, Philippi, Galatia, Thessalonica, and elsewhere formed the bedrock of Christian theological reflection, while theologians from Origen, Augustine, and Aquinas to the present time would elaborate and refine, dispute and codify, the ideas that Jesus put forward in the course of his tumultuous public ministry and through his Crucifixion and Resurrection.

Yet in its various forms, the essential message of Jesus, who became Christ — the Messiah — remains that of Mark 8:34, where he said with astounding simplicity: "If people wish to be my disciple, let them deny themselves and take up the cross and follow me." The nature of this cross may vary—in its weight and texture, its concrete horrors and degrees of agony—but its burden is beyond dispute. But so is the joy of reconciliation with God, with the exhilaration and comfort of Easter morning, which doesn't fade but continues to fill disciples of Jesus with zeal to repair a broken world, finding in his countenance the human glimmer of God's love. As the poet Gerard Manley Hopkins wrote so memorably, "I am all at once what Christ is, since he was what I am."[16]

8

The Afterlife of Jesus

Oh that I knew how all thy lights combine,
And the configurations of their glory!
Seeing not only how each verse does shine,
But all the constellations of the story.

— GEORGE HERBERT, "The Holy Scriptures"

The highest revelation is that God is in every man.

— RALPH WALDO EMERSON, *Journals*

Eyewitness Testimonies

FOR OVER TWO MILLENNIA, Jesus has attracted followers, has annoyed skeptics, and has baffled many who wonder what his existence meant, in all its wild paradox, as Bultmann recognizes when he writes, "The Christ occurrence means the eschatological occurrence through which God has put an end to the world and its history. There, this paradox is the claim that a historical event is at the same time the eschatological event."[1] That is, Jesus erases history, but he depends on it as well. As it were, the evolution of thinking about Jesus and what his existence signified began within moments of his departure from earth. Soon his disciples began to spread the gospel from Palestine outward, first colonizing adjacent territories, such as Macedonia and Thrace and Cappadocia, then taking the "good news" to Crete, Malta, Sicily, Egypt, and Rome, eventually reaching the farthest corners of the world. The church that arose in the name of Jesus splintered, however, into many churches, and some of these quarreled viciously, with competing theologies, all of them supposedly based on his life and teachings.

The most important early follower of Jesus was surely the apostle Paul. His letters, written twenty years or so after the Crucifixion, constitute the earliest Christian documents, composed two decades *before* the gospels themselves — a hugely important point that is rarely noted by Christians, who somehow imagine that because the Pauline epistles follow the gospels in the New Testament, they must have been written after them. (Thirteen of Paul's letters are found in the New Testament, although only seven are considered authentic; the others were written "in the tradition of Paul" by his associates.) Paul's supple and speculative mind shimmers through his correspondence, and it could easily be argued that he invented Christian theology by shaping its most elementary ideas. His formulations permeate all branches of the field to this day, and it seems impossible to imagine a Christian tradition of thought without him, even though others — James, the brother of Jesus, and Simon Peter, for instance — played huge roles in shaping the early church.

Stories about Jesus spread among his followers, and one assumes that those close to him — the eyewitnesses — could repeat versions of the Sermon on the Mount verbatim. The parables, too, would have traveled well. Stories of his encounters with people that he healed or comforted as he walked in Galilee would have been told and retold, and his final week in Jerusalem — his entry into the city on a donkey, the Last Supper, his arrest and trial, the Crucifixion and the Resurrection, with its astounding aftermath — would have riveted all who listened. That interested parties would write down these narratives was inevitable, and it's likely that we don't possess the earliest versions — the raw materials that the evangelists (canonical and otherwise) used for the gospels that, decades after Jesus, found their way into written form, in due course becoming the central documents of the New Testament.

The gospels purport to be eyewitness testimony. Think of the opening of Luke: "Given that many have undertaken to compile a story of the things which have been accomplished among us, and just as they were delivered to us by those who from the beginning were eyewitnesses and ministers of the word, it seemed wise to me, having followed all of these things closely for some time, to write an orderly account for you, most excellent Theophilus, that you may know the truth concerning the things of which you have been informed."[2]

This sounds very much like someone writing with personal knowledge of what happened, a writer with an urgent need to put down these "things that are most confidently believed among us." Richard Bauckham has argued convincingly that one can depend on the gospels as participating in the genre of historical memoir. These narratives, he says, "embody the testimony of the eyewitnesses, not of course without editing and interpretation, but in a way that is substantially faithful to how the eyewitnesses themselves told it, since the Evangelists were in more or less direct contact with eyewitnesses, not removed from them by a long process of anonymous transmission of the traditions."[3] Furthermore, Bauckham disputes the conventional (if unchallenged) view that "a long process of anonymous transmission in the communities intervened between their testimony and the writing of the Gospels." In other words, eyewitnesses wrote down what they knew rather quickly. They offered portraits of Jesus, not carefully detailed biographies, drawing on impressions, even word of mouth passed along by those present at the time of the events relayed.

Needless to say, for the gospels to be considered accurate memoirs one would have to take into account the complicated process of memory itself. Bauckham does so to a degree, citing recent psychological studies of memory. These widely accept that it's difficult to remember what happened last week, let alone a few decades ago. Memory plays tricks for all kinds of reasons, some innocent, others not so much. That is, sometimes a memory serves a purpose, semiconsciously, even unconsciously. One assumes that the evangelists each had a subjective view, an intended audience, with ideological assumptions that would have shaded their reflections.

Dale C. Allison, Jr. neatly summarizes the textual tradition of the New Testament: "Approximately 3,000 mss. of the Greek New Testament (part or whole) have been preserved, copied between the 2nd and 17th centuries, plus over 2,200 lectionary [manuscripts] containing sections (pericopes) of the New Testament arranged for reading in church liturgy from the 7th century on."[4] That is, no original manuscripts exist for the gospels, the letters of Paul, or any other material that appears in the New Testament. The first complete versions of the gospels, in fact, date to the fourth century—a very long time after the events they describe. One can only guess what the earlier versions might have looked like, or how scrupulous those who copied these texts might have been. (As there are numerous discrepancies in later copies of the gospels, one assumes that discrepancies happened along the way as well. Why wouldn't they?)

So many people rightly ask: Are these stories true? It's a complicated question without a simple answer. Pontius Pilate put the essential question before Jesus himself during his trial in Jerusalem: "So what is truth?" To a degree, literal truth isn't terribly hard to recognize. If I hit my thumb with a hammer, it hurts. That is true. If my father dies, I feel sad. That is true. Then again, even these simple examples have complications. I've hit my thumb many times with a hammer, as I like to play around with tools at home; yet I've hit my thumb fewer times in recent years. The pain of the first few strikes and black thumbs were necessary in the advancement of my carpentry skills. So context and personal history play a part in my understanding of this truth. When my own father died, I felt devastated. That was true. But he died over a decade ago, and though I continue to feel his presence in my life every day, and love him now as much as I did then, I — really and truly — don't miss him, not in the same way that I did at first. However odd, this is true as well.

Context is everything, and this makes it difficult to talk about the gospels, which are usually read out of context. Churchgoers like myself get used to hearing biblical texts recited in bits and pieces throughout the year. We hear passages from the Old Testament and the New. These fragments scatter in our heads and hearts, making it difficult to form a coherent picture, a sense of the overall pattern. And certain denominations — Christianity is a lush amalgam of churches and movements with very different theological opinions — tend to focus on one verse or another, highlighting a particular strain in the gospel narrative and repressing others. With the lectionary — the passages read in church each Sunday as stipulated by church authorities — an effort is made to link the readings, creating themes that reflect seasons in the church year, but the context is often lost on listeners.

In churches that run to the literal side, and where, in extreme cases, the Bible is taken as the Word of God in the most simplistic and literal fashion, certain verses stand out, summoned by pastors with flashing eyes, usually in the King James Version: "For the wages of sin is death; but the gift of God is eternal life through Jesus Christ our Lord" (Romans 6:23). Or "I am the way, the truth, and the life: no man cometh unto the Father, but by me" (John 14:6). These appear to narrow the path to heaven considerably, although a fuller exploration of such verses in their original Greek form often reveals a more complicated, and life-enhancing, message. In Matthew 7:13, for instance, Jesus famously says that the path to God is narrow but the gate is wide and the road broad that leads to destruction. This verse, and others like it, seem to fundamentalists to point to eternal damnation. Yet the word in Greek is *apoleia*, which often means "a sense of loss" or a "waste," thus mitigating the terror of endless torment so beloved of hellfire and brimstone preachers. The truth is, Jesus had little interest in damning anyone, and he certainly had no concept of hell as a place of perpetual torment.

A kind of literalist reading of the Bible came into play mainly in the wake of post-Enlightenment skepticism about scriptural texts, when a fierce reaction formed among a number of American and British preachers and scholars, who began to argue for biblical inerrancy, centering their faith on rather apocalyptic ideas teased mainly out of the Book of Revelation. One thinks of Dwight L. Moody, Charles Hodge, Arthur Pierson, Benjamin Warfield, or Cyrus I. Scofield in the U.S. or John Nelson Darby in England. Each of these men developed a large following, and to a degree their ideas still hold sway in Christian fundamentalist circles, with their emphasis on the end times, including the Second Coming and the Rapture, with the threat of hellfire and eternal damnation held up like a sword above the heads of fearful congregations. Belief in the inerrancy of the Bible gives them a sense of certainty that the modern age cannot offer.

Yet the Bible itself declared its openness to interpretation. In Hebrews 4:12 we read: "For the word of God is living and active." It's sharper than any "two-edged sword," piercing to the heart of a reader, "a discerner of the thoughts and intents of the heart." One has to accommodate all sorts of contradictory sayings and remarks by Jesus, Paul, and others. These often run against common sense, as in Luke 14:26: "If anyone comes to me and does not hate his father and mother, his wife and children, his brothers and sisters — yes, even his own life — he cannot be my disciple." Really? Didn't God in the Ten Commandments urge us to honor our father and our mother, and didn't Jesus in the Sermon on the Mount say that the commandments handed down to Moses remain firmly in place? A living and active reading of such passages draws us more fully into the text, into the living Word, which is unstable, always challenging, never set in stone.

The problem of translation complicates all readings of Holy Scripture, for a start. Jesus (and most of his disciples) spoke Aramaic, although one guesses he could read Hebrew as well, having been trained in a local synagogue in Nazareth — at least, one imagines this was the case. Yet the gospels unfold in a late form of Greek, aimed quite specifically at various groups within the early church, some of them Jewish and others gentile. The *Gospel of Thomas* comes to us in Coptic, like other early writings discovered in Egypt at Nag Hammadi in 1945. (It's impossible to know exactly what sources these Coptic translators drew on.) Many Jews at the time of Jesus knew the Hebrew Bible only in Aramaic translations called Targumim (a Targum is simply a translation) or in the widely influential rendition of the Old Testament into Greek known as the Septuagint, which dates from the third or second century BCE. So the story of Jesus takes on the colorations and idiomatic tones of many different languages. English versions, in fact, often derived from the popular Latin translation by Jerome, a very late (fourth century) version of the Bible commissioned by Pope Damasus I in 382, a translation that has many problems (and many glories as well).

Quests for the Historical Jesus

As for the historical details of the life of Christ, one feels the despair of scholars as they grapple with a long tradition known as the quest for the historical Jesus. Before the Enlightenment dawned in the late seventeenth century, there was not much concern about the historicity of the life of Christ: he was simply the man described in the four gospels. This was a world of superstition, where scientific inquiry had not quite impinged on theological matters. In the deist view of the world, popular in the eighteenth century, God was said to have created the clock of the universe, wound it tightly, and stepped aside to let it tick away. In the nineteenth century, a distinction arose between the Jesus of history and the Christ of faith, and this distinction has guided scholarship ever since, creating complications that remain difficult to address or "solve."

The first phase of the quest for the historical Jesus, called the Old Quest, began with Hermann Reimarus, a revered professor of theology at Hamburg in Germany. After his death, his most adventurous theological speculations found publication, including *On the Resurrection Narratives* (1777) — a nuclear bomb exploded in the midst of biblical scholarship. He considered Jesus a revolutionary with political designs on the Jewish community of Palestine and decided that his frantic disciples must have concocted the story of the Resurrection, after having first stolen his corpse from the tomb. He pointed to numerous contradictions in the gospel accounts, and he coolly exploited these differences. Various (mostly German) theologians followed in his rebellious wake, although some tried to reconcile the contradictions that Reimarus had raised. In 1835, David Friedrich Strauss published his *Life of Jesus Critically Examined*, bringing the historical problems in Jesus scholarship before a broad public and playing into Enlightenment skepticism that had grown over the past decades. He attempted to remove the supernatural parts of the narrative, as Thomas Jefferson had done before him, turning Jesus into an ethical philosopher, nothing more. He didn't see the gospels as history but legend, calling them myths — perhaps the introduction of that word into Christian discourse.

Strauss and successive theologians in Germany pioneered what became Source Criticism later in the century, centered on the idea that both Matthew and Luke drew on Mark as well as a lost document, always referred to as Q. What these scholars hammered home was that the first three gospels shared much the same vision, with many identical or nearly identical passages: hence, "Synoptic" came to describe them, as they saw the same things, even the same text. There could be no coincidence here. This was a case of rewriting and shaping existing material. These three gospels roughly tell the same story, with a few competing details, a few telling absences.

The results of source criticism became the norm, and nowadays few scholars dispute that Mark is the earliest of the gospels, or that Matthew and Luke follow him closely, drawing on additional material not available to Mark. John — the Fourth Gospel, as it's often called — continues to puzzle many, as it stands apart from its three cousins in style and substance. It presents new material (such as the story of Lazarus) and portrays a very different Jesus: one who does not, for instance, teach in parables but speaks broadly in "I am" statements, as in "I am the way, the truth, and the life." The majority of New Testament scholars date all four gospels to the second half of the first century, with Mark having been written about the time when the Second Temple was destroyed by the Romans in 70 CE. John was probably the latest, composed in the last decade of the first century, although a handful of scholars (including J. A. T. Robinson, a former Anglican bishop) place it much earlier, possibly before Mark. Robinson says, provocatively: "One of the oddest facts about the New Testament is that what on any showing would appear to be the single most datable and climactic event of the period — the fall of Jerusalem in 70 CE, and with it the collapse of institutional Judaism based on the temple — is never once mentioned as a past fact. It is, of course, predicted; and these predictions are, in some cases at least, assumed to be written (or written up) after the event."[5]

A huge amount of historical and textual study occurred in

the nineteenth century among Christian thinkers, culminating in Albert Schweitzer's justly famous *Quest of the Historical Jesus* (1906), which assembled all the known facts and relevant theories up to the date of its publication. At about the same time, other scholars, especially Johannes Weiss, began to dwell on the eschatological tone of the gospels, with their emphasis on a coming "end times" or *eschaton*. Schweitzer had picked up on this, observing the insistence on the end of the world in the gospels. Schweitzer argued that Jesus originally thought that a figure called the Son of Man would come and put an end to things. When this miraculous appearance or *parousia* failed to materialize, he simply became this figure himself, taking on a sacrificial role, imagining that his violent death would force the hand of God, who would bring all of history to a conclusion, with the righteous lifted up and the evil ones cast down. This didn't happen, so the Jesus of Schweitzer became a failure, a man who only managed to get himself crucified. In the famous last paragraph of his book, Schweitzer managed to lift the level of rhetoric to quite a feverish pitch:

> He comes to us as One unknown, without a name, as of old, by the lakeside. He came to those men who did not know who He was. He speaks to us the same word: "Follow thou me!" and sets us to the tasks which He has to fulfill for our time. He commands. And to those who obey him, whether they be wise or simple, He will reveal himself in the toils, the conflicts, and the sufferings which they shall pass through in His fellowship and, as an ineffable mystery, they shall learn in their own experience Who He is.[6]

In the wake of Schweitzer and several other major German theologians, Bultmann wrote in a moment of despair: "I do indeed think that we can know almost nothing concerning the life and personality of Jesus."[7] This provocative and now legendary statement was mainly a reaction to the late-nineteenth-century so-called Liberal Lives of Jesus, which sought to examine his psychology, as in the popular treatment of Jesus by Ernest Renan, whose *Life of Jesus* swept through Europe in the 1860s and continued to attract a wide audience for decades. But these biographies also reflected a growing awareness that much of the historical record was inaccessible, out of reach; it was impossible to know the details of Jesus's life in the way one knows the details of other historical phenomena. Instead of searching for some phantasm of history, Bultmann sought to discover the inherent message or *kerygma* of Christianity. With other colleagues, such as Hermann Gunkel, he developed what is called Form Criticism, a kind of "demythologizing" that seeks to discover a kernel of meaning within a particular form, such as a saying or a parable. Bultmann sought to take into account the setting for each narrative link in the gospels (German: *sitz im Leben*) in order to historicize it, to place it within a sound contextual framework.[8] He hoped to separate the mythic strands, grounding the story in scientific realities that "proceed from the world picture of natural science."[9] In doing so, he lost something of the mythic resonance of the narrative of Jesus, this *mythos* that I have hoped to reimagine.

The middle years of the twentieth century are often called the era of No Quest: scholars gave up on trying to locate Jesus in time and place, agreeing with Bultmann that the quest was whimsical. But massive discoveries of fresh material in mid-century brought a crisp wind from the Near East, especially with the uncovering of new texts, including the Gnostic Gospels at Nag Hammadi in Egypt in 1945 and the Dead Sea Scrolls in the late forties and fifties. As Cynthia Bourgeault says, "We're living in an era right now which some would call a major paradigm shift, where there's an opportunity as perhaps there hasn't been before to really open up the core questions again."[10] Already this was happening in the early fifties, when—fueled by these discoveries—interest in the life of Jesus picked up quite dramatically.

One of Bultmann's students, Ernst Käsemann, raised the issue of the quest once again in 1953, arguing that his teacher had been too skeptical concerning the historical evidence and that in the light of new evidence one must try to wed the Jesus of history with the Christ of faith. He raised the old specter of Docetism, an early heresy in which Jesus was regarded as wholly spiritual, never a human being who lived in historical time. One product of this reopening of the quest—often called the New Quest—was *Jesus of Nazareth* by Günter Bornkamm. Bornkamm wrote that each biographer of Jesus suffered from bringing "the spirit of his own age into his presentation of the figure of Jesus," usually with disastrous results. He concluded: "No one is any longer in the position to write a life of Jesus."[11] Nonetheless, he sought to lay down the undisputed facts, such as the birthplace of Jesus, his language (Aramaic), his baptism by John the Baptist, his trial and execution by the Romans. He emphasized the sayings of Jesus, the wise aphorisms that have traveled so well throughout the centuries. It turned out that one could count on quite a few hard facts, and that the sayings of Jesus could, after a fashion, often be judged as true statements. The quest was, once again, up and running.

A major effort to authenticate the sayings of Jesus began, with a lively group of scholars using various criteria of verification, such as "dissimilarity," wherein a saying was deemed true if it contradicted things that might have been said in Judaism or the early Christian church. In other words, if it sounded like something often said by rabbis, it probably wasn't something Jesus actually said. But this criterion has obvious problems. Why wouldn't Jesus simply repeat things that he'd heard in the local synagogues and considered worthwhile? There is the added difficulty that we know little enough about Judaic aphorisms during this period that it might be difficult even to know what was likely or unlikely as a saying.

Another criterion is multiple attestation. That is, a saying is more likely to belong to Jesus if it crops up in more than one place and it's not obvious that one source (Matthew or Luke) simply copied another (Mark). So scholars looked for multiple independent sources. Of course it makes sense that if different sources quote the same material, it might be especially noteworthy, even authentic. The problem is that it's difficult to know who copied what, or if oral tradition might have floated any number of sayings, which got picked up here and there, in canonical writings as well as texts that lay outside the canon.

There is also the criterion of embarrassment. Would Jesus really have said or done things that embarrassed him or his followers? If embarrassing things got reported in a gospel, they must be true, as the early church would not like to see them conveyed to potential converts — although they probably felt they must report something if it happened to be the truth. A famous example is that of the baptism of Jesus by John the Baptist. Why would the Lord himself require baptism? He was Jesus! And why would he submit to baptism by a lesser person? I myself see little value in this criterion. Good theological explanations exist for Jesus doing things like being baptized by John the Baptist or fraternizing with tax collectors and prostitutes. In addition, Jesus liked to shock people, as it proved a good way to get their attention. In addition to this, ethical behavior is often shocking, cutting against the grain of popular morality at any given time. And the writers of the gospels understood this.

The list of criteria used to authenticate the sayings of Jesus multiplied. Historical plausibility, for example, was another one that seemed to gather a lot of attention. A saying must actually seem in accord with things Jesus taught elsewhere if one were to consider it authentic. There were stylistic criteria as well; the saying must somehow "sound like" something Jesus might have said. That subjective or ideological distortions could play into such criteria seems obvious enough, and these distortions make it very hard to say with any certainty that a saying by Jesus was "true" or "false."

The next phase of Jesus studies, sometimes called the Third Quest, began in the 1980s, holding up the Jewish background of Jesus to close examination. This movement was aided by the discovery of the Dead Sea Scrolls as well as productive new archaeological digs in the region and the development of more sophisticated analyses of texts from the era. Scholars now reread Josephus as well as various rabbinical writings and newly discovered apocryphal texts in the light of freshly discovered facts. An explosion of research in the period of Second Temple Judaism helped to position the life of Jesus in a context that had explanatory value. Among those who pioneered this phase in Jesus studies were Géza Vermes, mentioned earlier, and E. P. Saunders, who published *Jesus and Judaism* in 1985 — an important point of reference for scholars interested in the Jewish origins of Christianity.

At about the same time as Vermes and Sanders began to explore the Jewish context of the gospels, the Jesus Seminar arrived on the scene, a group of 150 scholars founded in 1985 by Robert W. Funk under the auspices of the Westar Institute in Salem, Oregon. Among the leading members of the group were John Dominic Crossan, Marcus J. Borg, and Burton Mack. The group would meet twice a year to discuss the authenticity of sayings by Jesus, using criteria already in place and expanding on these with their own considerable skills in ancient languages and history. They used colored beads to vote on the degree of authenticity attached to each saying, for example, and voted by dropping them into a box. The Seminar rejected roughly eighty percent of the sayings by Jesus as either inauthentic or doubtful.

The danger of this approach is almost too plain and was nailed by Garry Wills, who wrote: "This is the new fundamentalism. It believes in the literal sense of the Bible—it just reduces the Bible to what it can take as literal quotation from Jesus. Though some people have called the Jesus Seminarists radical, they are actually very conservative. They tame the real radical, Jesus, cutting him down to their own size."[12] I would have to agree with Wills (whose various studies of Christian ideas have shaped my own thinking).

One interesting byproduct of the Jesus Seminar was *The Five Gospels* (1993), a retranslation of the canonical gospels, plus the *Gospel of Thomas*, by Funk, Roy W. Hoover, and other members of the Seminar.[13] This fresh translation of the Greek and Coptic texts is worth reading, even if one dismisses the idea of voting on the sayings of Jesus to determine their authenticity. In this edition, the sayings with a high degree of being the actual words of Jesus appear in red, those with less certainty appear in pink; those that seem like Jesus but are probably not his own words are gray. All sayings in black are considered as creations of his followers. While I find the project of trying to verify these sayings foolhardy, this edition provides thoughtful commentary and useful notes that explore the historical and literary aspects of given passages.

Despite the misguided efforts of the Jesus Seminar, there is much to admire in the Third Quest overall, a broad movement where Jesus emerges in a variety of forms, coming off as a millennial prophet (E. P. Sanders, John P. Meier, Dale C. Allison Jr.), as a revolutionary teacher (Marcus J. Borg), or as a political rebel wishing to overthrow both Herod Antipas and Rome (Richard A. Horsley, Reza Aslan). In other accounts, he becomes an itinerant rabbi who promulgated Kabbalah, a mystical form of Judaism (Bruce Chilton), or a radical Jew (Géza Vermes, Daniel Boyarin), or a master of ancient spiritual wisdom (Thich Nhat Hanh, Cynthia Bourgeault). In the many books by John Dominic Crossan, Jesus becomes a peripatetic Mediterranean peasant influenced by the Cynics — an early Greek school of philosophy that traced its origins back to Socrates; Crossan, in fact, tends to discount the historical nature of the gospel narratives, preferring to focus on their deeper meanings. In a recent study of the parables, for example, he concludes: "The *power* of Jesus's parables challenged and enabled his followers to co-create with God a world of justice and love, peace and nonviolence. The *power* of Jesus's historical life challenged his followers by proving at least one human being could cooperate fully with God."[14]

Finally, there is N. T. Wright, a former Anglican bishop who has written voluminously on the life and teachings of Jesus, notably in *Jesus and the Victory of God* (1996) and, more recently, *Surprised by Hope: Rethinking Heaven, the Resurrection, and the Mission of the Church* (2008). In a dialogue with Marcus J. Borg, Wright has gone to the center of his project as a scholar and Christian where he argues that historians are "not disembodied. He or she lives in the created world, the sacramental world, the human world, the political world, the world of a reality simultaneously mundane and shot through with glory." Once we have widened our horizons to include all this, he argues, "we will find, I believe, that the tension supposed to exist between history and faith is much more oblique, much less of a problem and more of a stimulus."[15] In effect, the problems dissolve as Jesus comes into view as an exemplary life, the human face of God, a mythic figure who lived in real time, transcending time.

The Meaning of Christ

That scholarship about Jesus should prove complicated, even contradictory, should surprise no one. Jesus was, and remains, a challenging figure, a voice that sounds through the centuries, calling us to attention, confronting us with hard truths as well as comforting words. He asks us to follow him. But the cost of discipleship, as Dietrich Bonhoeffer has shown us, is often high. In Bonhoeffer's case, the cost was his life itself: he died a martyr to the ideas he lived by. But he understood Christianity as not simply a set of doctrines, a list of "beliefs" that one must check off in order to be "saved." That wasn't Christianity at all. As Bonhoeffer writes, Jesus made it clear from the start "that his word is not an abstract doctrine ... but the re-creation of the whole life of man."[16]

That we can't quite grasp the full meaning of this message — the core message of Jesus — should come as no surprise. What does it mean, in fact, to call him the Incarnate Word, the *logos*, except to suggest that "God was in Christ" (II Corinthians 5:19), which is to say that the spirit of God moved in Jesus's life in order to accomplish God's purpose. The Incarnation, in other words, suggests that there was a spiritual presence in Jesus that was unique, bringing redemptive words into being, ushering forward deeds culminating in both the Crucifixion and the Resurrection. That such matters should prove difficult to comprehend with ordinary human intelligence should not surprise us.

Anything of real value requires an effort of understanding as well as dedication. But it's worth recalling that Jesus never meant to found a formal church with rituals and organized practices, to ordain priests, or to issue doctrinaire statements that formed a rigid program for salvation. Other than "follow me," his only commandment was "to love one another as I have loved you." He also asked us to break bread in his memory as a way of creating community, of extending the mystical body of Christ into the world at large. Most crucially, he wished for us to experience a change of heart — *metanoia* — a term which, as noted earlier, suggests a shift into a larger consciousness, a life-enhancing awareness of the mind of God, a deepening into fundamental layers of awareness that transforms and transports us, brings us into contact with profound realities. Jesus offered an invitation to everyone — to an awakening, to a sense of God-consciousness. This kingdom lies within us, in the soil of our creation.

I don't pretend to know more about Jesus than any well-disposed Christian who has spent a good deal of time reading about him, studying the Bible, trying to learn from his example and absorb the desert wisdom of his teaching. The place for anyone to begin their journey of faith is certainly with the gospels, including the *Gospel of Thomas*, with their rich layers of teaching and counsel, and with the letters of Paul, as well as other writings that have acquired sacramental value — as you will have gleaned, considerable portions of my own knowledge of religious ideas come from poetry itself, not only biblical poetry but a wide range of literature.

Revelation is active and ongoing, a lively stream that bubbles up from the ground of being. And the good news that Jesus hoped to spread continues to generate an endlessly active and emerging creation. As R. S. Thomas wrote in "Emerging"—

> *We are beginning to see*
> *now it is matter is the scaffolding*
> *of spirit; that the poem emerges*
> *from morphemes and phonemes; that*
> *as form in sculpture is the prisoner*
> *of the hard rock, so in everyday life*
> *it is the plain facts and natural happenings*
> *that conceal God and reveal him to us*
> *little by little under the mind's tooling.*

Acknowledgments

It would be impossible to acknowledge all of those who have helped me along my path over many decades in my pursuit of Jesus, but several friends read this manuscript in various drafts, including a number of gifted theologians and biblical scholars. These include Ellie Gebarowski Bagley, J. Stannard Baker, Edward Howells, Paul Jersild, John Kiess, Richard McLaughlan and O. Larry Yarbrough. Without their encouragement and suggestions, this book would have been infinitely poorer, although I accept full responsibility for all errors of fact and judgment. The manuscript was closely read by my editor and friend, James Atlas, and by my wife, Devon Jersild. Their suggestions were acutely intelligent and always helpful as well as encouraging.

Notes

Preface

1 Dietrich Bonhoeffer, *The Cost of Discipleship* (New York: Simon & Schuster, 1959), 33.

2 Bonhoeffer, 59.

3 Bonhoeffer, 55–56.

4 For a discussion of the Jewish context of Jesus, see Géza Vermes, *Jesus the Jew: A Historian's Reading of the Gospels* (London: Collins, 1973) or Daniel Boyarin, *The Jewish Gospels: The Story of the Jewish Christ* (New York: The New Press, 2012).

5 *Last Steps: The Late Writings of Leo Tolstoy*, ed. Jay Parini (London: Penguin, 2009), 164.

6 For a fuller discussion of *metanoia*, see Cynthia Bourgeault, *The Wisdom Jesus: Transforming Heart and Mind—a New Perspective on Christ and His Message* (Boston: Shambhala, 2008), 37–38. See also Murray A. Rae, *Kierkegaard's Vision of the Incarnation: By Faith Transformed* (New York: Oxford University Press, 1998). My reading of *metanoia* is also reinforced by Marcus J. Borg, *Jesus: Uncovering the Life, Teachings, and Relevance of a Religious Revolutionary* (San Francisco: HarperSanFrancisco, 2006), 219–20. Borg says: "The Greek roots of 'repent' mean 'to go beyond the mind that you have.'"

7 *The Gospel of Thomas: Wisdom of the Twin*, ed. Lynn Bauman (Ashland, Or: White Cloud Press, 2004), 8. I am grateful to Cynthia Bourgeault for directing me to this translation.

8 Dale C. Allison, Jr., *Constructing Jesus: Memory, Imagination, and History* (Grand Rapids, MI: Baker, 2010), 462.

9 Anselm of Canterbury, *Proslogion*, The Major Works, trans. M.J. Charlesworth (New York: Oxford University Press, 1998), 87.

1. Ancient Palestine

1 Bourgeault, 16.

2 See Jerry H. Bentley, *Old World Encounters: Cross-Cultural Contacts and Exchanges in Pre-Modern Times* (New York: Oxford University Press, 1993).

3 Joseph Campbell, *The Masks of God: Occidental Mythology* (New York: Viking, 1964), 397–98.

4 Joachim Jeremias, *Jerusalem at the Time of Jesus*, trans. F. H. and C. H. Cave (Philadelphia: Fortress Press, 1969), 22. This translation was based on the third German edition of this book, published in 1963.

5 Jeremias, 23.

6 Vermes, 62.

7 Jeremias, 251.

8 Simon Dubnow, *History of the Jews I* (South Brunswick, N.J.: T. Yoseloff, 1967), 74.

9 See Martin Hengel, *Jews, Greeks, and Barbarians: Aspects of the Hellenization of Judaism in the Pre-Christian Period*, trans. John Bowden (Philadelphia: Fortress Press, 1980). Hengel wrote numerous books on the Greek influence on early Christian thought and culture.

10 Boyarin, 5.

2. In the Beginning

1 The liturgy of the Christian church owes more to the Latin translation by Jerome than to the original Greek gospels, which were not widely known until long after many traditions and rituals hardened into formalities. Even most of the Church Fathers, including Augustine and Aquinas, knew very little Greek. It wasn't until the time of Erasmus and Luther, in the early sixteenth century, that it was taken for granted that a biblical scholar should go back to the original Greek for guidance.

2 The census is mentioned in Luke 2:1. The author takes pains to identify the time: it happened when Quirinius was governor of Syria. There are complex historical problems with the dating; but there was certainly a governor of Syria called Publius Sulpicius Quirinius (d. 21 ACE), who is mentioned in such ancient historians as Josephus, Suetonius, Tacitus, and Dio Cassius. This leads us to a further question: If the Christmas story here is "made up," why did the author take such pains to identify the historical setting? Perhaps the question answers itself. Veracity is im-

portant in a testimony, and the gospels are testimonial literature. The more specific the details, the more believable the story becomes. One added problem is that the census under Quirinius only related to the province of Judea, not those living in Galilee.

3 The phrase "Prince of Peace," commonly associated with Jesus, actually derives from a passage in Isaiah 9:6 in the Hebrew scriptures.

4 J. S. Bach's *Magnificat* (1723) is among the finest musical settings of this passage.

5 Vermes, 218.

6 Campbell, 336.

7 E. F. Burgess, "T. S. Eliot's 'The Journey of the Magi.'" *Explicator* 42 (Summer 1984), 36.

8 A Syrian commentator called Dionysius bar-Salbi, writing in the twelfth century, seems to have first suggested that Christmas was moved from January 6 to its present position because of the pagan Sol Invictus holiday. For a discussion of this and other theories about the dating of Christmas, see Thomas J. Tally, *Origins of the Liturgical Year* (Collegeville, MN: Liturgical Press, 1991).

9 From this, perhaps, follows the number of birds among the gifts given during the Twelve Days of Christmas, including the partridge in a pear tree!

10 This was quoted by Iraneaus of Lyon toward the end of the second century ACE. A similar gospel is the *Protoevangelium of James*, which has similar tales of the young Jesus. For a good survey of recent scholarship on the *Thomas* tradition and other non-canonical gospels, see: Simon Gathercole, *The Composition of the Gospel of Thomas: Original Language and Influences* (Cambridge: Cambridge University Press, 2012).

11 John P. Meier, *A Marginal Jew: The Roots of the Problem and the Person*, Vol. 1 (New York: Doubleday, 1991), 254.

3. The Dove Descending: His Ministry Begins

1 Vermes, 206.

2 Rowan Williams, *Arius: Heresy and Tradition*, 2nd ed. (Cambridge: Darton, Longman and Todd, 2002), 146.

3 Stephan J. Pfann, "The Essene Yearly Renewal Ceremony and the Bap-

tism of Repentance," in *The Provo International Conference on the Dead Sea Scrolls: Technological Innovations, New Texts, and Reformulated Issues*, eds. D. Parry and E. Ulrich (Leiden: Brill, 1999), 336.

4 Quoted in Stephen Hobhouse, *William Law and Eighteenth Century Quakerism* (London: G. Allen & Unwin, 1927), 240.

5 Joseph Campbell, *The Hero with a Thousand Faces* (Princeton: Princeton University Press, 1949), 23.

6 Biblical scholars generally agree that the language of Hebrews is not Pauline.

7 See Mark 3:21, for example.

8 Kenneth E. Bailey, *Jesus Through Middle Eastern Eyes: Cultural Studies in the Gospels* (Downers Grove, IL: InterVarsity Press, 2008), 154.

9 There is a minor cottage industry of books claiming to "prove" that Jesus was an Essene or closely allied with this devoutly ascetic group, which had a major outpost in the caves of Qumran. And the Dead Sea Scrolls reflect ideas similar to those we associate with Jesus.

10 See "A Faded Piece of Papyrus Refers to Jesus' Wife," by Laurie Goodstein in *The New York Times* (September 18, 2012). This fragment of papyrus was brought before the scholarly community by Professor Karen L. King of the Harvard Divinity School at the International Congress of Coptic Studies in Rome in September, 2012. Professor King herself has noted that this fragment proves nothing about the marital status of Jesus. It's nevertheless an intriguing bit of information from the ancient world, which suggests that questions about Jesus and his marital state could have been widespread in antiquity.

11 Thomas à Kempis, *The Imitation of Christ*, trans. Aloysius Croft and Harold Bolton (Mineola, NY: Dover, 2003), 139.

4. Walking in Galilee: The Healer and Teacher

1 See John 4:1–42, for the story in full. I compress and paraphrase.

2 I'm grateful to Cynthia Bourgeault for her reading of this episode in the life of Jesus in *The Wisdom Jesus*. My account draws on her throughout my discussion of this episode.

3 See Mark 3:22; Matthew 12:22–29; Luke 11:14–23.

4 See Wendy Cotter, "Miracle Stories, the God Asclepius, the Pythag-

orean Philosophers, and the Roman Rulers" in *The Historical Jesus in Context*, eds. A. J. Levine, D. C. Allison, and J. D. Crossan (Princeton: Princeton University Press, 2006), 166–78.

5 Wilde, of course, was referring to the English here; more broadly, I suspect, he referred to the English tendency to think in the reductively super-rational ways of empiricism and analytic philosophy.

6 See Vermes, 181. He notes that Rabbi Akiba, and many respected Jewish teachers, made all sorts of allowances for breaking the Sabbath when it was deemed humane or sensible. But the hostility in the gospels toward the Pharisees speaks to their date of compositions, decades after the death of Jesus, when Jews had taken firmly against the idea of Jesus as the Messiah. The Pharisees had replaced the Sadducees as the Temple elite by now, and they were therefore the establishment, so they needed bashing.

7 See Krister Stendahl, *The School of St. Matthew, and Its Use of the Old Testament*, 2nd ed. (Philadelphia, Fortress, 1968).

8 Joseph Ratzinger (Pope Benedict XVI), *Jesus of Nazareth* (San Francisco: Ignatius Press, 2007), 74.

9 Recounted by C. G. Jung in *Memories, Dreams, Reflections* (1963).

10 Liberation Theology arose from this first Beatitude, stressing the literal sense of the term "poor." Gustavo Gutiérrez, a Peruvian priest and theologian, published *A Theology of Liberation* in 1971, and he argued that Christ called his followers to pay close attention to those at the bottom of society. His writings have found a huge following in Latin America and Central America in particular. "The poor," he wrote, "are a byproduct of the system in which we live and for which we are responsible."

11 See Thich Nhat Hanh, *Living Buddha, Living Christ* (New York: Riverhead, 1995), 154. A Buddhist monk and renowned teacher, Nhat Hanh writes: "I do not think there is much difference between Christians and Buddhists. Most of the boundaries we have created between our two traditions are artificial. Truth has no boundaries."

12 Aristotle, *Nicomachian Ethics* 4.5.3. See Bailey, 73.

13 Rudolf Bultmann, *Theology of the New Testament* (New York: Scribner, 1955), 272.

14 Even if written *before* the fall of the Second Temple, these would have been stressful times for Jews within the boundaries of the Roman Em-

pire. Most scholars place the date of composition after the Temple was destroyed.

15 Wendell Berry, *The Unsettling of America: Culture & Agriculture* (San Francisco: Sierra Club Books, 1977), 122.

16 Berry, 120.

17 John P. Meier, *A Marginal Jew: Law and Love*, Vol. IV (New Haven: Yale University Press, 2009), 205–6.

18 I use a familiar version from the Anglican *Book of Common Prayer*.

19 Most Protestants use the doxology. Catholics (using the Latin Rite) do not. The doxology echoes a prayer found in I Chronicles 29:11: "Yours, O Lord, is the greatness and the power and glory." In the Greek and Byzantine liturgy, the priest usually sings the doxology.

20 For a thorough reading of The Lord's Prayer in the context of the Exodus story, see N. T. Wright, "The Lord's Prayer as a Paradigm for Christian Prayer," in *Into God's Presence: Prayer in the New Testament*, ed. Richard N. Longenecker (Grand Rapids, MI: Eerdmans, 2001), 132–54.

21 The word translated as "daily" in Greek (*epiousious*) is extremely rare, and it probably means "ongoing" or "continuing to be required" — translators have taken a stab at a decent English equivalent, and "daily" from the KJV seems as good as any. It has certainly lodged in the collective memory.

22 See Elaine Pagels, *Revelations: Visions, Prophecy, and Politics in the Book of Revelation.* (New York: Viking, 2012). It's not surprising that many early church leaders thought this book should not be included in the canonical New Testament. Even Martin Luther, early in his career, thought this apocalyptic vision had nothing to do with Christianity.

23 The Rosary is largely focused on a prayer to Mary that incorporates two verses from Luke: "Hail Mary, full of grace, the Lord is with thee. Blessed art thou among women, and blessed is the fruit of thy womb, Jesus. Holy Mary, Mother of God, pray for us sinners, now and in the hour of our death."

24 For a complete survey of this idea in world religions, see Jeffrey Wattles, *The Golden Rule* (New York: Oxford University Press, 1996). Wattles regards the "rule" as not the embodiment of a single idea but a concept that embraces growth on many levels.

25 This is David Hinton's translation.

26 This Babylonian code — the foundation of all Western law — was discovered in 1901.

27 It's interesting to note how many significant texts within Judaism emerged within a context of crisis and exile, such as the Lurianic Kabbalah in the late sixteenth century. Isaac Luria (1534–1572) was a mystic whose arcane writings attracted a huge following among exiled Jews — the Sephardim — who had been driven from Spain by Ferdinand and Isabella.

28 John Drury, *The Parables in the Gospels* (New York: Crossroad, 1985), 21.

29 Comical efforts to interpret this saying in ways that make it less difficult for the rich to swallow have appeared over the centuries, including the bogus idea that there was a gate in Jerusalem called "the camel," and that merchants had to unload their belongings to get through it. No such gate existed, alas. It may well be that the gospel saying turns on a misprint: *kamilos* (camel) in Greek could easily have been written as *kemêlos*, meaning cable or rope. In other words, it's easier to thread a needle with a rope than for a rich man to enter heaven. It's more probable, of course, that Jesus simply means that it's not easy for a rich man to enter heaven, given that "Blessed are the poor."

30 Drury, 60.

31 See C. H. Dodd, *The Parables of the Kingdom* (New York: Scribner, 1961) and Joachim Jeremias, *The Parables of Jesus*, trans. S. H. Hooke, 2nd ed. (New York: Scribner, 1954). Much of this work builds on the scholarship of Adolf Jülicher (1857–1938), who emphasized the central importance of the "kingdom of God" in the parables.

32 The basic Christian argument for belief in the miracles of Jesus will be found in C. S. Lewis, *Miracles* (London: Collins, 1947).

33 Ralph Waldo Emerson, "Self-Reliance."

5. Entering Jerusalem

1 See *Jesus and Archaeology*, ed. James H. Charlesworth (Cambridge: Eerdmans, 2006), for a useful selection of essays on recent archaeological work in this field.

2 The word *ekklesia* means "gathering," and only appears once more in the gospels, in Matthew 16:18. Roman Catholics interpret this declaration

as the initiation of apostolic succession. No other branch of Christianity makes this assumption.

3   Norman O. Brown, *Love's Body* (New York: Random House, 1966), 174. Brown was a classical scholar and philosopher who, in the sixties, became an iconic figure in countercultural circles. He is largely forgotten today, but his eccentric, prophetic work repays close reading.

4   See Mark 14:3–11. The Temple Scroll from the Dead Sea Scrolls also refers to a village east of Jerusalem where the sick are cared for. This was probably Bethany.

5   In the Hebrew scriptures, both Elisha and Elijah raised people from the dead. See I Kings 17:17–24 and II Kings 4:32–37.

6   See Morton Smith, *Clement of Alexandria and a Secret Gospel of Mark* (Cambridge: Harvard University Press, 1973). Smith, as a young professor at Columbia, claimed to have discovered a letter from Clement (an early Church Father) that, among other things, described a very different version of the Lazarus story in a "secret" version of Mark. Recent scholars have questioned the authenticity of this letter. See, for example, Stephen C. Carlson, *Morton Smith's Invention of Secret Mark* (Waco: Baylor University Press, 2005).

7   The parallels between Jesus's raising of Lazarus and the Egyptian myth of Osiris having been raised by Horus are intriguing.

8   John P. Meier, *A Marginal Jew: Mentor, Message, and Miracles*, Vol. II (New York: Doubleday, 1994), 798–99.

9   Yerushalayim, a Hebrew name for this site, means something like "God sees the whole, or the peace." Peace is *Salem* or *Shalem*, as in Genesis 14:18. The Greeks called the city Hierosoylma, and *hiero* means holy in Greek. The first written instance of the city name occurs on a parchment buried in a cave near the town of Lachish dating from the sixth century BCE.

10 One should also consider Luke 13:6–9, where Jesus tells a parable about a fig tree. A man wants to cut it down, but another says: "Leave it alone for one more year, and I'll dig around it. If it bears fruit next year, fine! If not, I'll cut it down." The symbolic aspect lies in the metaphor of pruning.

11 John Howard Yoder, *The Politics of Jesus: Vicit Agnus Noster* (Grand Rapids, MI: Wm. B. Eerdmans, 1972), 185.

12 See Lawrence H. Shiffman, From *Text to Tradition: A History of Judaism in Second Temple and Rabbinic Times* (Jerusalem: Ktav, 1991). Recent scholars have questioned whether, in the time of Jesus, the Sanhedrin met in a regular way. He might, for example, simply have been called before a smaller group of elders.

13 Leonardo depicts the moment when Jesus said that one of his disciples would betray him. Each disciple reacts in his singular way, with shock or disbelief registered in subtle ways.

14 Whether or not the Last Supper was actually a *seder* remains in dispute. Mark suggests this, and Matthew and Luke agree. John, however, sees this meal as taking place during the Day of Preparation. For John, Jesus becomes a sacrificial, or paschal, lamb, and lambs were sacrificed on the Day of Preparation. It's a slight difference but suggests that competing theologies were already in place in the late first century.

15 Raymond E. Brown, *An Introduction to the New Testament* (New York: Doubleday, 1997), 289.

16 Paul Tillich, *The Courage to Be* (New Haven: Yale University Press, 1952).

17 See Paul Tillich, *The Eternal Now* (New York: Scribner, 1963).

6. The Passion: From Gethsemene to Golgotha

1 Quoted in Pagels, 74.

2 A great deal of speculation surrounds this idea of which exact scriptures Jesus, in his self-sacrifice, fulfills. There is the image of the suffering servant in Isaiah 53 and the righteous sufferer in Psalm 22. Others point to the last six chapters of Zechariah. For an overview of this subject, see Stephen P. Ahearne-Kroll, *The Psalms of Lament in Mark's Passion: Jesus' Davidic Suffering* (Cambridge: Cambridge University Press, 2007).

3 Erich Auerbach, *Mimesis: The Representation of Reality in Western Literature*, trans. Willard R. Trask (Princeton: Princeton University Press, 1953), 45.

4 Early manuscripts in Greek supply the first name of Barabbas as Yoshua — which translates as Jesus. Scholars have long noted the parallels between the names of Jesus Barabbas and Jesus Christ.

5 See his well-known *On the Embassy to Gaius*, readily available online.

6 The historicity of the kind of crucifixion described in the gospels has been confirmed by archaeological finds. In 1968, for example, the remains of a body crucified in a manner similar to Christ was found at Giv'at ha-Mivtar in northeast Jerusalem.

7 Mark, Matthew, and John call it Golgotha, probably based on the Hebrew word for skull (*gulggolet*).

8 Bauckham, *Jesus and the Eyewitnesses: The Gospels as Eyewitness Testimony* (Grand Rapids, MI: Eerdmans, 2006), 505.

9 It is widely assumed by scholars that Hebrews, while reflecting many of the apostle Paul's ideas, was not written by him. The Greek is much more elevated in style than his Greek, more formal, and does not adhere to the usual epistolary forms that Paul favored. It might have been a sermon based on one of Paul's sermons but written by an especially articulate scribe.

10 There are several ancient references to strange happenings when Julius Caesar died. See Plutarch's *Lives*, Chapter 69, or Virgil's First Georgic, where he writes: "The sun took pity on Rome when Caesar died / And covered his brilliant face in sooty dark." My attention was drawn to the lines in *Hamlet* by A. N. Wilson.

11 He is described as an "honorable counselor" in Luke 23:50, translating the Greek word *bouleutes*, sometimes used to refer to a member of the Sanhedrin.

12 Luke 24:53.

13 See Peter Abelard, "The Cross" in *Sermons*, 12. Quoted by Pelikan, 106.

7. Resurrection

1 See John Dominic Crossan, *Jesus: A Revolutionary Biography* (San Francisco: HarperSanFrancisco, 1995). Crossan argues that most people — political rebels, many of them — were not buried after having been crucified by Romans in the first century. They were left to hang to terrify the population, who might harbor among them other revolutionaries. But this does not constitute an argument that Jesus was not properly buried. The burial is mentioned in every gospel as well as in I Corinthians 15:3–4. And Pilate might well, as suggested above, have had political

reasons for allowing the body to be buried. There was the added influence of two members of the Sanhedrin.

2 For a full discussion of this hypothesis, see Dale C. Allen, *Resurrecting Jesus: The Earliest Christian Tradition and its Interpreters* (New York: T & T Clark, 2005), 352–62.

3 In 1968, archaeologists discovered the remains of one Yehohanan, who had been buried after a crucifixion. A four-and-a-half inch nail was still lodged in one ankle. One hears about burying convicts during religious festivals in both Philo and Josephus. See Helen K. Bond, *The Historical Jesus: A Guide for the Perplexed* (London and New York: T & T Clark, 2012), 164.

4 Alan E. Lewis, *Between Cross and Resurrection: A Theology of Holy Saturday* (Grand Rapids, MI: Eerdmans, 2003), 42. For a full discussion of Lewis in relation to the poetry of R. S. Thomas, see Richard McClaughlan, "R. S. Thomas: Poet of Holy Saturday" in *The Heythrop Journal*, v. 52, Issue 6 (November 2011), 976.

5 McClaughlan, 985.

6 Pagels, 64.

7 Rudolf Otto, *The Idea of the Holy*, 2nd ed., trans. John W. Harvey (New York: Oxford University Press, 1950), 34. See also Melissa Raphael, *Rudolf Otto and the Concept of Holiness* (Oxford: Clarendon Press, 1997).

8 I'm not so much contradicting Bultmann's idea of demythologization as putting the emphasis more firmly on the balance between literal and figurative readings, while stressing the fictive aspect: the shaping spirit of the gospel narratives.

9 See, for example, Jason B. Hood, "The Cross in the New Testament: Two Theses in Conversation with Recent Literature (2000–2007)," *Westminster Theological Journal* 71 (2009), 281–95. A survey of the footnotes here alone reveals a vast literature on the subject.

10 *The Asian Journal of Thomas Merton*, eds. Naomi Burton, Patrick Hart, and James Laughlin (New York: New Directions, 1973), 233.

11 See Acts 1:9–11, Mark 16:19, and Luke 24:50–53 for accounts of the Ascension, which are very brief.

12 One grows tired of hearing fundamentalist preachers digging into dream-like passages in Revelation and connecting dots that cannot connect. I often wish they would heed the good advice offered in the Book

of Job, where God says: "If you have anything to say, say it." He adds: "If
not, hold your peace" (Job 33:32–33).

13 Josephus, *Antiquities* 18.16

14 Brown, 283–84.

15 Reinhold Niebuhr, *The Nature and Destiny of Man*, v. II (Louisville,
    KY: John Knox Press, 1996), 294. This major, two-volume work origi-
    nally appeared in 1943.

16 From "That Nature is a Heraclitean Fire and the comfort of the
    Resurrection."

8. The Afterlife of Jesus

1 Rudolf Bultmann, *New Testament and Mythology and Other Basic Writings*, ed. and trans. Schubert M. Ogden (Philadelphia: Fortress Press,
   1984), 163.

2 The addressee, one Theophilus, remains unknown; but his name in
   Greek means "lover of God," so it's possible that this was a generic ad-
   dress, composed with a wry smile, a wink of acknowledgment to those
   who consider themselves lovers of God. Here as throughout this book,
   I use my own versions of the New Testament, except where the King
   James Version (KJV) is so well known that it seems pointless to erase
   it. With quotations from the Old Testament, I generally use the King
   James Version, except where clarity is at stake.

3 Bauckham, 6.

4 Allison, 48.

5 John A. T. Robinson, *Redating the New Testament* (London: SCM
   Press, 1976), 13.

6 Albert Schweitzer, *The Quest of the Historical Jesus*, trans. W. Montgom-
   ery (London: A & C Black, 1954), 401.

7 Rudolf Bultmann, *Jesus and the Word* (London: Ivor Nicholson and
   Watson, 1935), 14.

8 See Bultmann, *New Testament and Mythology*. See also *History and Eschatology: The Presence of Eternity* (New York: Harper and Row, 1962).

9 Bultmann, *New Testament and Mythology*, 5. For a full description of
   Bultmann's idea of demythologization, see Robert C. Roberts, *Rudolf
   Bultmann's Theology: A Critical Interpretation* (Grand Rapids, MI:
   Wm. B. Eerdmans, 1976).

10 Bourgeault, 3–4.

11 Günter Bornkamm, *Jesus of Nazareth* (New York: Harper, 1960), 1. Originally published in German in 1956.

12 Garry Wills, *What Jesus Meant* (New York: Viking, 2006), xxv.

13 *The Five Gospels: The Search for the Authentic Words of Jesus*, trans. with commentary by Robert W. Funk, Roy W. Hoover, and the Jesus Seminar (New York: Macmillan, 1993).

14 John Dominic Crossan, *The Power of Parable: How Fiction by Jesus Became Fiction about Jesus* (New York: HarperCollins, 2012).

15 Marcus J. Borg and N. T. Wright, *The Meaning of Jesus: Two Visions* (New York: HarperCollins, 1999), 227–28.

16 Bonhoeffer, 62.

Select Bibliography

The literature on Jesus is daunting, and I refer to more books and articles in this book than I cite below. But the following are the books that I kept close at hand while working on this project. Many of them have been old friends over many decades. Some are recent additions to my library. I referred to them often as I wrote this study.

Allison, Dale C. , Jr. *Jesus of Nazareth: Millenarian Prophet*. Minneapolis: Fortress, 1998.

—— *Constructing Jesus: Memory, Imagination, and History*. Grand Rapids: Baker Academic, 2010.

Armstrong, Karen. *A History of God: The 4,000 Year Quest of Judaism, Christianity, and Islam*. New York: Knopf, 1993.

—— *The Bible: A Biography*. New York: Atlantic Monthly Press, 2007.

Barnstone, Willis and Marvin Meyer, eds. *The Essential Gnostic Scriptures*. Boston: Shambhala, 2010.

Bauckham, Richard. *Jesus and the Eyewitnesses: The Gospels as Eyewitness Testimony*. Grand Rapids, MI: Wm. B. Eerdmans, 2006.

Beilby, James K. and Paul Rhodes Eddy, eds. *The Historical Jesus: Five Views*. Downers Grove, IL: IVP Academic, 2009.

Bond, Helen K. *The Historical Jesus: A Guide for the Perplexed*. London: T & T Clark, 2012.

Borg, Marcus J. *Meeting Jesus Again for the First Time*. New York: HarperCollins, 1994.

——with N. T. Wright. *The Meaning of Jesus: Two Visions*. New York: HarperOne, 1998.

Bourgeault, Cynthia. *The Wisdom Jesus: Transforming Heart and Mind—a New Perspective on Christ and His Message*. Boston: Shambhala, 2008.

Boyarin, Daniel. *The Jewish Gospels: The Story of the Jewish Christ*. New York: The New Press, 2012.

Brown, Raymond E. *An Introduction to the New Testament.* New York: Doubleday, 1997.

Bultmann, Rudolf. *Theology of the New Testament.* New York, Scribner, 1955.

—— *New Testament & Mythology and Other Basic Writings.* Trans. Schubert M. Ogden. Philadelphia: Fortress, 1984.

Charlesworth, James D. *Jesus and Archaeology.* Grand Rapids: Wm. B. Eerdmans, 2006.

Chilton, Bruce. *Rabbi Jesus: The Jewish Life and Teaching that Inspired Christianity.* New York: Doubleday, 2000.

Crossan, James Dominic. *The Historical Jesus: The Life of a Jewish Mediterranean Peasant.* San Francisco: HarperCollins, 1991.

—— *The Power of Parable: How Fiction by Jesus Became Fiction about Jesus.* New York: HarperCollins, 2012.

Drury, John. *The Parables in the Gospels.* New York: Crossroad, 1985.

Funk, Robert W., Roy W. Hoover, and the Jesus Seminar. *The Five Gospels: The Search for the Authentic Words of Jesus.* New York: Macmillan, 1993.

Jeremias, Joachim. *Jerusalem in the Time of Jesus.* Philadelphia: Fortress, 1969.

Levine, Amy-Jill, Dale C. Allison, Jr., and John Dominic Crossan, eds. *The Historical Jesus in Context.* Princeton: Princeton University Press, 2006.

MacCulloch, Diarmaid. *Christianity: The First Three Thousand Years.* New York: Penguin, 2009.

Meier, John P. *A Marginal Jew: Rethinking the Historical Jesus: The Roots of the Problem and the Person,* Vol 1. New York: Doubleday, 1991.

—— *A Marginal Jew: Rethinking the Historical Jesus: Mentor, Message and Miracles,* Vol 2. New York: Doubleday, 1994.

—— *A Marginal Jew: Rethinking the Historical Jesus: Companions and Competitor,* Vol 3. New York: Doubleday, 2001.

—— *A Marginal Jew: Rethinking the Historical Jesus: Law and Love,* Vol 4. New Haven: Yale University Press, 2007.

Otto, Rudolf. *The Idea of the Holy.* Trans. John W. Harvey. New York: Oxford University Press, 1923.

Pagels, Elaine: *The Gnostic Gospels.* New York: Random House, 1979.

—— *Revelations: Visions, Prophecy, and Politics in the Book of Revelation.* New York: Viking, 2012.

Pelikan, Jaroslav. *Jesus Through the Centuries: His Place in the History of Culture.* New Haven: Yale University Press, 1985.

Ratzinger, Joseph (Pope Benedict XVI). *Jesus of Nazareth.* San Francisco: Ignatius Press, 2007.

Sanders, E. P. *Jesus and Judaism.* London: SCM, 1985.

Tillich, Paul. *The Courage to Be.* New Haven: Yale University Press, 1952.

—— *The Dynamics of Faith.* New York: Harper & Row, 1957.

Vermes, Géza. *Jesus the Jew: A Historian's Reading of the Gospels.* London: Collins, 1973.

—— *Jesus in the Jewish World.* London: SCM, 2010.

Wills, Garry. *What Jesus Meant.* New York: Penguin, 2006.

—— *What the Gospels Meant.* New York: Penguin, 2008.

Wilson, A. N. *Jesus: A Life.* New York: Norton, 1972.

Wright, N. T. *How God Became King: The Forgotten Story of the Gospels.* New York: HarperOne, 2012.

—— *Jesus and the Victory of God.* London: SPCK, 1996.

—— *The Resurrection of the Son of God.* Minneapolis: Fortress, 2003.

—— *Surprised by Hope: Rethinking Heaven, the Resurrection, and the Victory of Christ.* New York: HarperOne, 2008.

—— *Who Was Jesus?* London: SPCK, 1992.